Sweet & Natural Baking

Sweet & Natural Baking

Sugar-Free, Flavorful Recipes from Mäni's Bakery

Mäni Niall

Photography by Mark McLane

CHRONICLE BOOKS

SAN FRANCISCO

Library of Congress Cataloging-in-Publication Data available.

ISBN 0-8118-1049-6

Printed in Hong Kong.
Designed by Michael Osborne Design
Food and prop styling by Danielle Di Salvo

Distributed in Canada by Raincoast Books
8680 Cambie Street
Vancouver, B.C. V6P 6M9

10 9 8 7 6 5 4 3 2 1

Chronicle Books
275 Fifth Street
San Francisco, CA 94103

Contents

Acknowledgments *8*

How to Love Desserts with a Clear Conscience *9*

Low Fat versus Nonfat *12*

The Sweet and Natural Pantry *15*
    Sweeteners *16*
    Flour *18*
    Other Ingredients *21*
    Fruit Juice Reduction *23*
    Prune Butter *23*

Breakfast Treats *25*
    Sticky Pecan-Raisin Buns *26*
    Faux-Nuts *28*
    Southern-style Cornmeal Waffles *29*
    Apple Streusel Coffee Cake *30*
    Baked Apples with Maple-Pecan Crust *32*
    Blueberry Buttermilk Pancakes *33*
    Banana-Nut Pancakes *34*
    Banana-Pecan Scones *37*
    Cranberry-Walnut Scones *38*
    Fresh Strawberry Scones *40*
    Barley-Currant Scones *41*

Mäni's Muffins *43*
    Blueberry Corn Muffins *45*
    Chocolate-Walnut Muffins *46*
    Oil-Free Cornmeal Muffins *48*
    Blueberry–Oat Bran Muffins *49*
    Huckleberry-Apple Muffins *50*
    Washington State Blackberry Muffins *51*

Raspberry–Oat Flour Muffins *52*
Carrot-Pineapple Muffins *54*
Peach–Poppy Seed Muffins *55*
Banana-Walnut Muffins *56*
Raisin Bran Muffins *57*

The Cookie Jar *59*

Chocolate Chip and Pecan Cookies *61*
Deep Dark Brownies *62*
Chocolate-dipped Barley Cookies *64*
Granola Triple Oat Cookies *65*
Chocolate Truffle Heart Cookies *66*
Applesauce-Currant Cookies *68*
Almond Jewel Cookies *69*
Butter Spritz Cookies *70*
Coconut Macaroons *71*
Raspberry Linzer Cookies *72*
Almond Shortbread *74*
Ginger Happy Face Cookies *75*
Red Hot Peanut Butter Cookies *76*
Lemon Poppy Gems *77*

A Celebration of Cakes *79*

Black Forest Bundt Cake *82*
Banana Layer Cake with Cream Cheese Frosting *83*
Blackberry Upside-Down Cake *84*
Chocolate Raspberry Fortress Cake *86*
Modern Mini Fruitcakes *88*
Hollywood Cheesecake *90*
Chunky Carrot Cake *91*
Mocha Almond Cake *92*
Strawberry Shortcakes with Mäni's Special Strawberry Sauce *95*

Upper Crust Pies and Tarts *97*
(plus Turnovers and a Cobbler, too)

New-Fashioned Pie Dough *98*

Apple Turnovers *99*

Peach Foldover Pie *100*

Apple–Pecan Praline Tart *102*

Apple Tart with Yogurt Custard in a Walnut-Oat Crust *103*

Pear Frangipane Tart *104*

Apple-Blueberry Double Crust Pie *106*

Pumpkin-Yam Pie *107*

Apple-Cherry Cobbler *108*

Fresh Strawberry Tartlets *110*

Lemon Meringue Tartlets *111*

Cool and Natural *113*

Tropical Fruit Mousse Parfait *115*

Vanilla Bean Ice Milk *116*

Strawberry-Banana Ice Milk *118*

Pineapple Frozen Yogurt *119*

Blood Orange Sherbet *119*

Pink Grapefruit Sorbet *120*

Two-Berry Granita *120*

Strawberry Custard Cups *121*

Mäni's Sugar-Free Truffles *122*

Nutritional Analysis by Recipe *125*

Index *129*

Table of Equivalents *132*

Acknowledgments

THIS BOOK NEVER WOULD HAVE BEEN POSSIBLE if Mäni's Bakery didn't exist first. And I never would have undertaken the project of starting the bakery without the participation and encouragement of my business partner, Larry Maiman. Thanks for recognizing a good sugar-free dessert when you tasted one! Many other people also contributed in crucial ways during our company's infancy: James Jaffee, Arnold Elser, Tara Matson-Jonaitis, Trish Gallaher, Danny DeVito, Haines Wilkerson, Denise Wakeman, Amanda Killian, Chris Wypiski, Larry Turner, Mary Coller, Mark and Melissa McLane, and Mike Browning. Thanks also go out to Barbara Durbin, Susan Derecskey, Danielle Di Salvo, and Michael Osborne.

A special thanks to Michael Jackson for showing me that any dream can be achieved: All you have to do is believe. And do the work.

A special thanks to my Mom and Dad for letting me play in the kitchen, and to sister Karing for allowing me to make a mess and mistakes in her kitchen when I was in high school. I first sensed the excitement of food through my dear friend Akasha. We tasted great food together in the Los Angeles kitchens of Wolfgang Puck, Michael Roberts, and Nancy Silverton, and on trips to the San Francisco Bay Area to enjoy the restaurants Greens at Fort Mason and Chez Panisse.

I am grateful to Bill LeBlond and everyone at Chronicle Books for making this book a reality and to Judith Weber, who believed in the project from the start. I am indebted to Rick Rodgers for all his help in making my baking style "user friendly." Thanks to the California Prune Board and *Eating Well* magazine for giving me the impetus to create more low-fat desserts and to the California Strawberry Board for the sweetest strawberries ever.

How to Love Desserts
with a Clear Conscience

FOR SEVERAL YEARS NOW, I have created magnificent muffins, mouth-watering cakes, flaky pies filled with juicy fruits, European-style tarts, old-fashioned turnovers, luscious chocolate truffles, and other delectable treats that have won rave reviews with both confirmed dessert hedonists and health-conscious hardliners. These people are my customers at Mäni's Bakery, where they have found that they do not have to sacrifice flavor for healthful eating. At Mäni's, all the desserts are totally free of refined sugars and are made with organically grown flour and other all natural ingredients.

More and more Americans are acknowledging the huge role food plays in the quality of their lifestyle, and have cut out ingredients that have an adverse effect on their well-being. Sometimes my customers have been told by their doctors of food allergies or intolerances to such foods as wheat, dairy products, eggs, or sugar, but just as often they have evolved to their own personal food choices. I live and work in Los Angeles, where many of my desserts' biggest fans are in the entertainment industry, and they scrutinize every fat gram they consume. All these people agree that a satisfying dessert lifts the spirit, and if made with minimally processed ingredients, can fortify both the body and mind. Simply put, enjoying well-made, healthful food makes you feel better.

Some people come to a more healthful lifestyle when faced with a threatening crisis, like a heart attack or serious allergy. I was lucky—I came to appreciate this kind of cooking because I liked it. At Verde Valley school in Sedona, Arizona, in the seventies, a number of students were vegetarian, and we were allowed to cook our own meals. I loved the nights I was head cook, experimenting and learning from my favorite natural foods cookbooks. One night, I made eggplant parmesan for the entire school, and when they all told me how great it was, a professional cook was born. I made a spiritual journey to India, and when I returned, I took a job in a vegetarian restaurant. Soon I had become chef and had added a bakery and catering business. From there I enjoyed a stint as Michael Jackson's personal chef, traveling all over the world preparing his vegetarian meals, followed by a tour of duty at the Nowhere Café in Los Angeles. Eventually I opened Mäni's Bakery with my business partner, Larry Maiman. As soon as the media heard about my creating baked, all-natural, sugar-free doughnuts as a prop for Danny DeVito in a movie, Mäni's Bakery became the place to get desserts that combined good health with good taste. All along, I wanted to bake fresh and healthful desserts that would capture the taste buds and imagination in the same way that the California cuisine of Wolfgang Puck and Alice Waters awakened my senses.

This is not a diet cookbook. The term sugar free is not in an equation with low calorie, and although you will find many recipes here that are reduced fat, my emphasis is on making good-looking, good-tasting desserts with minimally processed natural ingredients. Most of our foods today are overprocessed and lack the wholesome flavor of the food before it was improved with chemicals and technology. Sugar is one of the saddest examples of this tragedy.

Human beings have only four basic taste sensations: sweet, sour, bitter, and salty. Considering the alternatives, it is no surprise that humankind has always preferred sweet things. Very sweet fruits like berries, figs, and dates figure prominently in ancient literature. An Egyptian hieroglyph of a bee exists from around 4000 B.C., and the Bible gives sweets the seal of approval when it refers to the promised land as flowing with milk and honey. Honey was used as the primary sweetener in Europe until the sixteenth century. Sugar was available, but only to the very rich for a princely sum. Mainly used as a medicine, sugar was monopolized by the Arab countries, making it difficult to obtain. Efforts to grow sugarcane on mainland Europe always failed. During the Age of Discovery, it was found that sugarcane prospered in the New World, and sugar literally poured into Europe. The public quickly indulged its sweet tooth, first adding spoonfuls of sugar to their beverages and before long purchasing the new confections developed by bakers and candymakers. In 1700, the average English person consumed four pounds of sugar per year—by 1780, the amount had tripled to twelve pounds.

In less than three hundred years, a relatively unknown food has become a major part of our diet. Now, in most affluent countries, the per capita consumption is around one hundred pounds per person! Americans get twenty to twenty-five percent of their calories from sugar. That's way too much. All nutritionists agree it does absolutely nothing for your health and should be avoided whenever possible.

Before refining and processing, sugarcane contains such nutrients as calcium, phosphorus, iron, potassium, vitamin E and the B vitamins, pantothenic acid, thiamine, riboflavin and niacin, along with such minerals as copper, iron manganese, and zinc. By the time the sugarcane juice reaches your kitchen pristinely white and glistening (after being clarified, boiled, crystallized, put through a centrifuge, redissolved, decolorized and recrystallized), all of its nutrition has been destroyed. That's why sugar is said to be empty calories.

Raw sugar, brown sugar, and honey have all been touted as healthier choices, but in reality, they have all been processed to varying degrees. True raw sugar is unfit for human consumption; it contains remnants of the sugarcane plants and is dirty with soil. Turbinado and other raw sugars are actually only slight variations on the traditional sugar refining process. Brown sugar is actually made from white sugar with molasses (itself a by-product of sugar refining) added back into it. Honey is refined nectar, and the bees remove most of the nutrients almost as effectively as man's machines, even if the process is considered a natural one.

None of the desserts in this book use refined sugars. Instead, I rely on less refined natural sweeteners like liquid fruit juice concentrate and granulated maple syrup (which is commonly sold as maple sugar). Small amounts of honey are used in only a few recipes as a flavoring agent, not as the major sweetener. To me, the biggest appeal of using fruit sweeteners is that they are less removed from their original state than other sweeteners. With liquid fruit juice concentrate, my favorite sweetener, the fruit is juiced and reduced to a higher concentration by a vacuum process; it is sometimes pasteurized. That's it—the refining process is complete. I hate cloying desserts that are dominated by the taste of white sugar. Fruit juice concentrates are not as sweet as sugar, allowing the natural flavors of the ingredients to shine. But choosing a minimally processed sweetener is only one aspect of making healthful desserts. I use as many whole-grain flours as possible, lots of fruits and nuts to add both flavor and texture, and fruit purees to substitute for part of the fat when I want to create a reduced-fat dessert.

Americans have a new awareness about their food. New laws regarding labeling and recommendations regarding fat content are all evidence of this trend. Yet experience has proven to me that people will not sacrifice the pleasure of eating simply for health reasons. *Sweet and Natural Baking* allows you to create magnificent desserts by combining traditional pastry techniques with minimally processed and refined ingredients, bridging the gap between health concerns and great-tasting food. I strive to combine the latest health information with the rich and varied history of culinary tradition to arrive at a truly satisfying cuisine. No compromises have been made—these desserts are attractive and mouth-watering. For people who have cut out certain foods from their diets to help their well-being, I have recipes for egg-, dairy-, and wheat-free desserts and quite a number of reduced-fat desserts, too. Indulging in a sweet should be a treat. Don't look at dessert as a vitamin pill or as preventive medicine—make it a worthwhile part of a complete, balanced diet.

Low Fat versus Nonfat

As I've said, this is not a diet cookbook. At Mäni's Bakery, we developed a following because we offer a huge variety of desserts for everyone, regardless of their culinary lifestyle or dietary restrictions. Granted, our low-fat desserts get a lot of positive feedback, but it's because they taste good, not just because they have a low fat content. My criterion for a successful dessert is how it tastes, not how much or how little fat it contains. If it doesn't taste good, people won't buy it.

I think that the American consumer has gone fat-free crazy. Remember the anticholesterol campaign, or the sodium scare, or when oat bran was touted as the miracle food? I am thrilled that people are interested in healthier eating, but I wish every trend would not be blown out of proportion. The worst part is that as soon as the trend has peaked, any good information that came from it is considered passé until the next revelation comes along. There always seems to be a recurring theme: Too much of any food is bad for you. It's no secret that moderation and balance in diet are the key, and exercise must be used in conjunction with good eating in order to maintain a healthy lifestyle.

Admittedly, the American diet is much too fatty, and the average eater should look for ways to trim the fat. Note that I say *trim* the fat, not eliminate it completely. Fat, along with prote in and cholesterol, is a necessary macronutrient for a healthy body. But less than 30 percent of our daily caloric intake should come from fat—some nutritionists and doctors say even this is too high and recommend 20 or even 10 percent—whereas most Americans average about 37 percent fat intake and above.

When I began experimenting with low-fat baking, my first results were not too encouraging. I overreacted to the warnings about fat just like many other consumers and tried to banish fat from many of my recipes. I admit that I compromised on taste, thinking, "Gee, I guess this is what low-fat desserts are supposed to taste like and if they're good for you, that's the trade-off." When I put these well-intentioned nonfat desserts out on the bakery shelves, the customers voted with their wallets: The desserts sold out the first couple of days, but few customers bought them again.

I went back to the drawing board. It didn't take me long to see that my mistake was in trimming too much fat from the recipes. In the pastry kitchen, butter (and other fats), eggs, and sweeteners are building blocks, the basis of all dessert creations. Cutting out fat entirely is like telling an artist he or she can paint only with a third of the palette. I discovered that fruit purees were truly wonderful fat substitutes (especially prune butter), but I got the best results when I combined them with a minimum amount of fat. Gradually I started using the low-fat techniques that are now part of a baker's vocabulary: using low-fat or skim milk instead of regular, substituting egg whites for whole eggs (but often leaving a yolk or two in the recipe to add moisture), replacing sour cream with nonfat yogurt or buttermilk (which in spite of its name is a low-fat product), using chunks of fruit to add texture to batters, heightening flavors with a grating of lemon or orange zest.

In some baked goods in this book I have not added any fat to the recipes other than that found naturally in the ingredients. These are exceptions to my usual skepticism towards nonfat baked goods. Oil-Free Cornmeal Muffins are fantastic served warm from the oven, spread with fruit-sweetened fruit spreads. On the other hand, there are indulgences like the buttercream-frosted Mocha Almond Cake, which would make any celebration special. Remember, the key is moderation and balance— if you have the cake at a birthday party, your next dessert should be low fat, that's all, or you should exercise a little bit harder the next day.

There is an important caveat about so-called fat-free desserts. Commercially produced and packaged foods achieve their coveted nonfat status in two ways. First, they use ingredients that contain no fat. Sometimes these products, such as sugar and egg whites, are naturally fat free, or like nonfat sour cream, they are harmless nonfat versions of a fatty food. But more often they are manmade food substitutes that simulate, but never equal, the qualities of real food. Secondly, the suggested portions on the back of the box are often unrealistically tiny. According to the U.S. Department of Agriculture (USDA), any food that contains less than $1/2$ gram of fat gets the green light as a nonfat food. Companies manipulate the portion size until it is small enough to fit into this category. At Mäni's Bakery, our hearty portions alone would keep them from being labeled fat free, according to USDA standards.

I believe that fat free is nothing but a marketing term, ignoring the traces of fat naturally found in the ingredients. "No Added Fat," the term we use at the bakery, is a much more realistic designation. If you are trying to bake desserts at home that have the same qualities as the "No Fat!" desserts you see at the supermarket, you'd better give up. Those things—I can't really call them desserts—are processed by an unnatural, chemical-laden technology that just isn't applicable in the home kitchen, and I must say, I hope never is.

The Sweet and Natural Pantry

One of the truest culinary axioms is that a finished dish will only be as good as the ingredients. Since the ingredients used in these recipes are minimally processed, your desserts will be much better for you than those made with overprocessed, nutritionally barren foods. In this chapter ingredients that may be new to your kitchen are explained and clarified, and included are a couple of basic recipes for homemade versions. Although all of the ingredients are available at natural foods stores and many supermarkets (or, if you are lucky enough to have one in your area, a natural foods superstore), I have given mail order sources, too.

Sweeteners

Liquid fruit juice concentrate

This syrupy sweetener is the most versatile of sugar substitutes, and I use it in most of my recipes. Various fruit juices are vacuum processed and reduced to a honeylike consistency, bursting with the fruit's flavor and just mildly sweet with a slight tang. Fruit juice concentrates are much less removed from their natural state than other sweeteners. Sugar tends to dominate the flavor of any preparation it is used in, but since fruit juices are not as sweet as sugar, baking with juice concentrates allows the natural flavors in the dessert to shine. In the last few years, fruit juice concentrate has become a popular commercial sweetener, used in fruit spreads, cereals, cookies, muffins, sodas, and candies.

Fruit Sweet

The brand name of my favorite commercially available liquid fruit juice concentrate. Fruit Sweet is reddish gold in color, a well-balanced blend of peach, pineapple, and pear juices. It is similar to the industrial fruit juice concentrate blend we use at Mäni's Bakery, and it is one of the secrets of our success. Most natural foods bakeries use white grape juice concentrate, which is easier to find, but I prefer the mellower, more complex taste of the peach-pineapple-pear blend.

For best results, use Fruit Sweet in the recipes in this book. It is sold nationwide in most health food stores and some groceries. It is available by mail order from Wax Orchards, 22744 Wax Orchards Road, S.W., Vashon Island, WA 98070 (1-800-634-6132).

White grape juice concentrate

The same consistency as Fruit Sweet and almost the same sweetness threshold. It is dark brown in color. White grape juice concentrate is not the same thing as the purple grape version, which is too sour to use in baking. It is my second choice for a minimally processed sweetener. Mail order from Wax Orchards or from Walnut Acres, Penns Creek, PA 17862 (1-800-433-3998).

Other flavors of liquid fruit juice concentrate

Also found at natural foods stores. Not all of them are right for dessert making. Apple juice concentrate is the most widely available variety and can be used in a pinch. However, it is more tart than Fruit Sweet or white grape juice concentrate, so don't expect your desserts to be as sweet. Avoid cranberry, cherry, and purple grape juice concentrates—they are too acidic to be used in desserts, although they can be reconstituted according to the package directions for excellent unsweetened beverages. Not only will these fruit concentrate flavors make the desserts taste too sour and give them an odd color, the acid content will throw off the proportions of baking powder and baking soda. (These leavenings are alkalis, and react with the acid in a recipe to create carbon dioxide, which makes the batter rise. If the acid-alkali ratio is thrown off in a recipe, the leavening's chemical reaction will malfunction, and the batter will not rise properly.)

Frozen white grape or apple juice concentrate

Found in the frozen food section of the supermarket. These can be transformed into liquid fruit juice concentrate at home. I've seen many recipes that simply call for substituting these thawed supermarket juice concentrates for liquid fruit juice concentrates, but I find that this doesn't work very well. The supermarket concentrates are too thin. By boiling them down on the stove or in a microwave oven, they can be thickened to the proper viscosity and the flavor will be intensified. This is a very simple procedure, outlined in the recipe for Fruit Juice Reduction (page 23). You may find it the most economical way to supply your kitchen with liquid fruit juice concentrate.

Unsweetened organic fruit juices

These can also be boiled down to make liquid fruit juice concentrate from scratch. It takes about 20 minutes to reduce one quart of juice to one cup, which should have the proper syrupy consistency. However, the results will not be as consistent as using Fruit Sweet, white grape juice concentrate, or the Fruit Juice Reduction, so I don't recommend this until you are familiar enough with the viscosity of the other versions to make a comparison. I did not test any recipes with from-scratch reductions, but I want you to be familiar with the possibility. Be sure to buy unsweetened organic fruit juices—pear, peach, and apple are good choices. You could also use freshly squeezed juice in an extreme case, but, again, I can't guarantee total success. If you use these homemade sweeteners, enter into your recipe making with a spirit of adventure and experimentation.

Some recipes call for cooking the fruit juice concentrate in a nonreactive saucepan, that is, stainless steel or enamel-lined. Some metals, such as aluminum or cast iron, will react when they come in contact with an acidic ingredient like fruit juice concentrate, imparting their color and a metallic taste. Most modern saucepans are nonreactive, but be careful if you prefer to use older pots.

Maple sugar

This is maple syrup that has been dehydrated to a granular texture similar to supermarket granulated brown sugar. It is less sweet than refined sugar and adds a hint of mellow maple flavor to desserts. Not only is it a wonderful baking ingredient, it is handy to keep in a sugar bowl to sprinkle on unsweetened breakfast cereals or fresh fruit or to stir into beverages. Maple sugar can be reconstituted with hot water to make instant maple syrup for your pancakes and waffles. You may find it in natural foods stores in small bottles labeled maple sprinkles, granulated maple syrup, or powdered maple. It can be pricey, so try to buy it in bulk to keep the price down. Be sure it is all maple; sometimes it has been blended with other sugars to make a cheaper product. It can be mail ordered from The Vermont Country Store Catalogue, Weston, VT 05255 (1-802-362-2400).

Flour

All wheat flours contain varying amounts of gluten, a protein that affects the texture of the final product. Gluten creates a mesh-like web in a dough that can catch the gases created during leavening, allowing the dough to rise. Wheat is the only grain that contains enough gluten to make doughs strong enough to rise. Although rye also has a small amount, it must be combined with wheat flour to make a light-textured product. Choosing a wheat flour with the proper gluten content will affect the texture of your baked goods. Depending on the type of wheat planted, the resulting flour will be hard (with a high gluten content) or soft (with a low gluten content). There are two kinds of wheat flour, whole wheat and white. Whole wheat flour has all of the bran and germ retained during milling; white flour has the bran and germ removed and is often chemically bleached.

Since the bleaching process strips away nutrients, I never cook with bleached flours. When you bake with whole-grain flours, you are bringing more minerals, vitamins and fiber into your diet. Whole-grain flours contain vegetable protein (which is much less expensive to produce than animal protein), complex carbohydrates, B vitamins, and iron. They are usually low in fat and have a high proportion of dietary fiber. Another advantage is that many of these flours are often organic, produced with environmentally sound methods without the use of synthetic pesticides or fertilizers. Store all opened whole-grain flours in the refrigerator, since the lack of processing makes it easy for them to turn rancid at room temperature. Keep them wrapped in plastic bags to keep out unwanted refrigerator odors. Whole-grain flours can be found at natural foods stores and many supermarkets, or from Walnut Acres (page 16) or Arrowhead Mills, Box 2059, Hereford, TX 79045 (1-800-749-0730), or from my favorite source, which is the brand used at Mäni's Bakery, Giusto's Vita Grain Flour Mills, 241 E. Harris Ave., South San Francisco, CA 94080 (1-415-873-6566).

The proper measurement of flour is a controversial subject among food professionals. Some believe that the flour should be spooned (or in some instances, sifted) into a measuring cup, and then leveled with a knife. At the bakery, where we work in large quantities, it is most convenient to weigh out the flour. In Europe, home cooks weigh all of their ingredients on kitchen scales. However, I have found that the vast majority of American home cooks measure by the dip and scoop method, and that is how these recipes were tested.

To dip and scoop, use the proper measuring cup. Do not use a glass measuring cup with a lip, which is for liquid ingredients. Dry ingredient measuring cups come nested in $1/4$-, $1/3$-, $1/2$-, and l-cup sizes. Dip the appropriate cup into the flour (in its bag or a container) and use a knife to level off the excess flour at the top of the cup. In this book, all of the flours are measured first, then sifted.

When baking with whole-grain flours, the batters are naturally a darker brown color than those made with all-white flour. This makes it problematic to use the expression, "Bake until the top is golden brown." I try to give you more specific tactile and visual tests for doneness, like testing with a toothpick, watching for the edges of the cake to shrink from the sides of the pan, pressing the tops of cookies with a finger to see if they are solid enough to spring back, and so on.

I use three types of wheat flour in this book:

Unbleached all-purpose flour

Made from high-gluten hard wheat. This is used primarily in yeast breads, but because sweeteners and fats have a tenderizing effect on flour, it is often used in cakes and cookies, too. Unbleached all-purpose flour is normally available in bulk at natural foods stores and cooperatives.

Whole wheat pastry flour

A low-gluten, soft wheat flour. This makes excellent cakes, quick breads, cookies, muffins, and pie crusts. Whole wheat pastry flour contains most of the bran and germ of the wheat; it has a light brown, speckled appearance. Do not confuse it with regular whole wheat flour, a high-gluten ingredient that is not used in this book. Like unbleached all-purpose flour, look for whole wheat pastry flour in bulk.

Soft unbleached pastry flour

A somewhat new product on the shelves. Pale beige in color, it is similar to bleached all-purpose flour in that it creates very tender pie crusts, shortcakes, and other baked goods, but it has been left blessedly unbleached. Made from soft wheat, it has had the bran and germ removed, so I like to bolster its nutritive value by mixing it with whole wheat pastry or other grain flours. By combining soft white pastry flour with other whole grains, you can avoid the heavy texture that sometimes accompanies natural baked goods. Look for the Arrowhead Mills brand in 1¼-pound sacks in a natural foods store. Walnut Acres has a similar low-gluten flour called All-Purpose Flour Blend. Both can be mail ordered (pages 16 and 18).

Oat flour and barley flour

I use these flours to create wheat-free sweets for gluten-intolerant dessert lovers. The flours have a natural sweetness and a slightly nutty taste that can be very appealing. Because these flours don't contain the protein gluten that gives structure to doughs, though, they need a little special attention:

🐜 Aerate the ingredients in a wheat-free dough to be sure the baked goods don't end up heavy or stodgy.

🐜 Aerate the flour with the other dry ingredients by sifting into a bowl.

🐜 Beat wet ingredients with a handheld electric mixer until very frothy with air bubbles.

🐜 Stir the dough just until it comes together; don't overmix.

You may also choose to mix oat or barley flour with wheat flour to give another dimension to your baked desserts. Do not substitute more than one-fourth of these whole-grain flours for the wheat flour, though, or the dessert will have a heavy texture.

How to substitute gluten-free flours

If you want to experiment with gluten-free flours in your baked goods, it is better to resort to the European method of weighing the flour on a kitchen scale, since each whole-grain flour has a different density, making the American way of measuring by volume unreliable. Weigh the measured amount of white flour called for in the recipe (it normally weighs about 5 ounces per cup measured by the dip and scoop method). Substitute an equal weight of gluten-free whole-grain flour. You will get better results baking small wheat-free desserts like cookies and muffins. The denser texture caused by lack of gluten is more noticeable in larger desserts.

Other Ingredients

Bran

The outer husk of a grain, removed during processing. Wheat and oat bran are easily available at natural foods stores. I mix bran into some doughs to add flavor, nutrition, and fiber, not because some people believe oat bran lowers cholesterol blood levels. Wheat and oat bran are interchangeable; the difference in their flavor is negligible. Store bran in a covered container in the refrigerator.

Fruit purees

Can stand in for part of the saturated fats in many baked goods. Note that I said "part of" the saturated fats. I find that few people like completely fat-free baked desserts, myself included. Unsweetened applesauce and mashed ripe bananas are two purees that work well, but there is another fruit puree that is really big news, prune puree.

Prune puree is probably the best chemical-free fat replacement ever discovered. Certain varieties of plums are dried to become prunes, and these can be blended into a butterlike consistency. Remarkably, prune puree has many of the same baking qualities as such saturated fats as butter or vegetable shortening. Prune puree's consistency allows air to be beaten in during the creaming step, giving the baked goods an excellent texture. The malic acid, sorbitol, and pectin found in the prunes prevent gluten from forming. (A gluten strong dough is desirable in bread, but gluten development should be discouraged in tender baked goods.) Prunes are also a natural humectant; they absorb moisture and give low-fat cookies and cakes a moist, melt-in-your-mouth quality that is missing from the spongy, tough textures of many low-fat desserts.

Supermarkets carry prune butter, also called lekvar, but it is usually loaded with refined sweeteners. Unsweetened prune butters are available at some natural foods stores, but Prune Butter (page 23) is so easy to make at home in a food processor, I don't see any advantage to buying a prepared product.

Fruit-sweetened fruit spreads

These have a flavor and texture similiar to fruit jams and preserves, but because they are sweetened with fruit juice concentrate instead of sugar, the fruit flavors really shine. (According to the USDA, jams or preserves must contain sugar, and since fruit spreads are sugar free, they must be called by another name.) I use fruit spreads for cake and cookie fillings and glazes for pies, tarts, and cheesecakes. Found in super-markets and natural foods stores, they come in such flavors as apricot (often melted and used as a glaze), strawberry, and blueberry.

Malt-sweetened semisweet chocolate chips

Made without refined sugars or dairy products. Unsweetened, semisweet, and bitter-sweet chocolates never have dairy products, but white and milk chocolates do. Look closely at the labeling to be sure you are not buying unsweetened chips. My favorite brand is Sunspire.

How to melt chocolate chips

Place the chips in a bowl or the top part of a double boiler set over very hot—not simmering—water, and stir occasionally until melted. Do not melt these chips in a microwave oven, or they may scorch. Malt-sweetened chips will have a thicker vis-cosity than refined sugar-sweetened chips. If you plan to dip cookies or truffles, thin the melted chocolate with 1 teaspoon vegetable oil for each 1 cup (6 ounces) of chips. Malt-sweetened semisweet chocolate chips are available from Sunspire, 2114 Adams Avenue, San Leandro, CA 94577 (1-510-569-9731).

Soy milk

Available plain, as a soy–rice milk blend, and either sweetened (with fruit juices or malt) or unsweetened. It is also available in low-fat versions. I prefer the sweetened kind, especially for those unaccustomed to the taste of soy milk. It is not so highly sweetened that it will affect the sweetness in the recipe, but you can use unsweetened soy milk if you prefer. Soy milk can be substituted for regular, low-fat, or nonfat milk products in baked recipes. However, if the soy milk is to be heated, as in the Soy Milk Truffles (page 124), be sure to heat the soy milk gently and do not let it boil, or it will curdle. If you are substituting soy milk for buttermilk, add 2 teaspoons of lemon juice or vinegar to the wet ingredients to simulate buttermilk's acidity.

Tofu

Also known as bean curd. Tofu comes in soft, firm, and extra-firm textures. It is an excellent source of protein, and I use it in dairy-free desserts to give a creamy, thick texture without cream. I like to buy the 10¼-ounce aseptically packed boxes of Mori-Nu brand, stored at room temperature on the grocery shelf. You can also purchase it stored in water and refrigerated in the produce section. The recipes in this book call for firm tofu; the weights are always for drained amounts.

Fruit Juice Reduction

Makes 1 cup

Boiling supermarket juice concentrate until syrupy will allow you to make your own liquid fruit concentrate at home without a trip to the natural foods store. The juice reduction must be completely cool before using, so make this the very first thing you do when preparing a recipe. The reduction can be simmering away while you are preheating the oven, greasing pans, and measuring other ingredients, and you won't waste any time.

The fruit juice reduction can be prepared in larger quantities, in proportionately larger utensils. For example, two 12-ounce containers of frozen apple juice will yield 2 cups of apple juice reduction, but make it in a larger saucepan or a 2-quart measuring cup to avoid boiling over.

12 ounces frozen white grape juice or apple juice concentrate, unthawed

To make on the stove: Place the unthawed juice concentrate in a wide medium heavy-bottomed saucepan and bring to a full boil over high heat. Boil rapidly until the liquid is reduced to 1 cup, about 10 minutes. Pour the liquid into a glass measuring cup to measure accurately.

To make in the microwave: Place the unthawed juice concentrate in a 1-quart microwave-safe container. A 1-quart glass measuring cup works best, as you can use the increments on the side of the cup to check how much the liquid has reduced. Microwave on High (100%) until the liquid has reduced to 1 cup, about 12 minutes. This recipe was tested in a 700-watt oven; if yours has a lower wattage, it will take longer. Cool completely before using. To speed cooling, pour the reduction into a medium bowl placed in a large bowl full of iced water. Stir often until cooled and slightly thickened, about 10 minutes. The fruit juice reduction will keep, covered and refrigerated, for up to 1 week. Bring refrigerated fruit juice reduction to room temperature before using.

Prune Butter

Makes 2 cups

As soon as I started using prune butter in many of my low-fat desserts, I became a convert. You can make just as much as you need for a recipe following the proportions of three parts pitted prunes to one part hot water, by volume—the amount of pitted prunes used will yield the same amount of puree. (For example, one cup prunes pureed with one-third cup water yields one cup puree.) However, since the prune butter keeps for up to two weeks in the refrigerator, make a big batch for convenience's sake. Measure prune butter in a metal measuring cup, leveling off the top. It is too loose to measure accurately in a glass liquid measuring cup.

2 cups (9 ounces) pitted prunes

⅔ cup boiling water

In a food processor fitted with the metal blade or in a blender, chop the prunes. With the machine running, pour the water through the feed tube. Continue running the machine until the mixture is smooth, 2 to 3 minutes. Stop the machine occasionally and scrape down the sides. There will be a few small chunks of prune left unpureed, which is fine. The prune butter will keep, covered and refrigerated, for up to 2 weeks.

Breakfast Treats

Mornings are a busy time at Mäni's Bakery, as people stop in on their way to work to pick up something to nibble on. They have quite a choice—scones, coffee cake, our famous Faux-Nuts, and muffins. I often find bakery offerings too sweet for the first thing in the morning, but these treats allow our customers' bodies to warm up gently, without the sugar-shock of the gooey stuff found in the display case of a doughnut shop. It will be a hard decision to choose what recipes to bake from this chapter. All decisions should be this pleasurable.

In this chapter, I also include breakfast favorites that we don't serve at the bakery, such as pancakes, waffles, and baked apples. It is a special treat to lounge around the breakfast table enjoying a steaming plate of pancakes or waffles doused with maple syrup or topped with berries. (Use both and you'll use less syrup.) On busy mornings, I am happy to provide my customers with their breakfast on the run. I just hope that on not-so-busy mornings they occasionally stay home to relax and smell the waffles . . . I mean, roses.

Faux-Nuts

Sticky Pecan-Raisin Buns

Egg Free

Makes 8 buns

Sticky buns in a sugar-free cookbook? Sure—fruit juice concentrate makes a great gooey sauce for these wonderful rolls. They are incredible when served warm, but for the best flavor, let them cool for about 20 minutes before you break down and attack them. You could burn your mouth easily on the hot syrup.

DOUGH

1 cup milk

2 tablespoons liquid fruit juice concentrate or Fruit Juice Reduction (page 23)

2 tablespoons unsalted butter, cut into small pieces

1 envelope active dry yeast (scant 2½ teaspoons)

1½ cups unbleached all-purpose flour, plus more as needed

1 cup whole wheat pastry flour

½ teaspoon fine sea salt

SYRUP

4 tablespoons (½ stick) unsalted butter

⅔ cup liquid fruit juice concentrate or Fruit Juice Reduction (page 23)

1 tablespoon ground cinnamon

1 tablespoon heavy cream

Butter, for the pan

1 cup (4 ounces) pecan halves

1 cup raisins

1 tablespoon unsalted butter, melted

1 **To make the dough:** In a medium saucepan, heat the milk until small bubbles appear around the surface. Remove from the heat and add the fruit juice concentrate and butter. Let cool until tepid (100° to 110° F.). Stir well. Sprinkle with the yeast and let stand 5 minutes. Stir to dissolve the yeast.

2 In a large bowl, whisk the unbleached and whole wheat pastry flours with the salt to combine. Make a well in the center and add the milk mixture. Stir to form a soft, sticky dough. On a floured work surface, knead the dough, adding additional flour as needed, until supple and elastic, about 8 minutes.

3 Place the dough in a well-buttered medium bowl and turn to coat the dough. Cover with plastic wrap and place in a warm spot. Let stand until the dough has almost doubled in volume and a finger pressed ½ inch into the dough leaves an impression, about 1 hour.

4 **To make the syrup:** In a small nonreactive saucepan, melt the butter over medium heat. Add the fruit juice concentrate and cinnamon and bring to a simmer. Reduce the heat to low. Cook, stirring constantly, until the mixture becomes a thick syrup with big bubbles on the surface, 2 to 3 minutes. Remove from the heat, stir in the cream and let stand until tepid, about 20 minutes. The syrup should be cool enough to spread without running.

5 Position a rack in the center of the oven and preheat the oven to 375° F. Butter well a 9 x 3-inch springform pan. Sprinkle the pecans in the bottom of the pan.

6 Punch down the dough. On an unfloured work surface, roll or pat out the dough to a 9 x 12-inch rectangle. Spread the syrup over the dough, leaving a 1-inch border at the top. Sprinkle the raisins over the syrup. Starting at a long end, roll up the dough into a thick cylinder. Using a sharp knife, cut the dough crosswise into 1½-inch-thick slices. Place cut side down in the prepared pan.

7 Cover the pan with plastic wrap and place in a warm spot. Let stand until the dough has almost doubled in volume, about 45 minutes.

8 Brush the tops of the buns with the melted butter. Bake until the tops are browned and the sauce is bubbling in the center, 30 to 35 minutes. Cool in the pan on a wire cake rack for 5 minutes. Invert the buns onto a serving platter and remove the sides and bottom of the pan. Scrape any nuts and syrup clinging to the bottom of the pan onto the buns. Cool for at least 20 minutes before serving warm.

Faux-Nuts

Whole Grain

Makes 12 Faux-Nuts

Here they are, the "doughnuts" that made Mäni's Bakery famous. Faux-Nuts were the answer to a cry for help from Danny DeVito during the filming of a movie. Danny's character was addicted to doughnuts, and Danny was required to eat massive quantities during the takes. In reality, Danny does not consume sugar or fried foods. So I created a simple fruit juice-sweetened banana muffin, baked it in the shape of a doughnut and rolled it in various glazes and toppings. These fakes, dubbed Faux-Nuts by my friend Mary Coller, were such a hit with Danny and the crew that we quickly added them to our daily repertoire at the bakery.

Nonstick vegetable oil cooking spray and all-purpose flour, for preparing pans

3 cups whole wheat pastry flour

1½ teaspoons baking soda

1½ teaspoons ground cinnamon

½ teaspoon fine sea salt

1¾ cups mashed ripe bananas (about 4 medium bananas)

3 large eggs

1¾ cups plus 1 cup liquid fruit juice concentrate or Fruit Juice Reduction (page 23), divided

¼ cup canola oil

¼ cup buttermilk

2 teaspoons vanilla extract

Shredded unsweetened coconut, chopped nuts, graham cracker crumbs, grated chocolate, or dried currants, for toppings

1 Position a rack in the center of the oven and preheat the oven to 350° F. Lightly spray the insides of twelve 4-inch mini bundt pans with nonstick vegetable oil spray, then sprinkle with all-purpose flour and tap out the excess.

2 Sift together the whole wheat pastry flour, baking soda, cinnamon, and salt into a large bowl and make a well in the center.

3 In a medium bowl, using a handheld electric mixer set on medium-high speed, beat the mashed bananas and eggs until smooth, about 1 minute. Add *1¾ cups* of the fruit juice concentrate, the oil, buttermilk, and vanilla and beat for 2 minutes. Pour into the well and beat for 2 minutes, scraping down the sides of the bowl as needed. Pour the batter into the prepared pans, filling no more than three-fourths full. This is easiest to do by transferring the batter to a large glass liquid measuring cup.

4 Bake until a toothpick inserted in a cake comes out clean, 15 to 18 minutes. Cool on a wire cake rack for 10 minutes. Invert the pans and rap against the work surface to unmold. Cool completely, right side up, on the wire rack.

5 Meanwhile, in a small saucepan, bring the *remaining 1 cup* of fruit juice concentrate to a boil over medium-high heat. Remove from the heat and pour into a small, deep bowl.

6 Place each of your chosen toppings in a small bowl. One at a time, invert a Faux-Nut and dip briefly into the concentrate, then roll in the desired topping. Repeat with the remaining Faux-Nuts. (Leftover fruit juice concentrate can be strained to remove any stray crumbs and saved for another use.)

Chocolate-dipped Faux-Nuts: In the top part of a double boiler or in a heat-proof bowl set over hot, not simmering water, melt 2 cups (12 ounces) malt-sweetened semisweet chocolate chips with 1½ teaspoons vegetable oil, stirring until smooth. Remove the top part of the double boiler from the bottom and cool the chocolate slightly. Tilt the bowl so the chocolate collects in a deep pool. Invert a Faux-Nut and dip into the chocolate, letting the excess chocolate drip back into the bowl. Shake the Faux-Nut gently to remove excess chocolate, if necessary. Place on a baking sheet and refrigerate briefly to set the glaze.

Southern-style Cornmeal Waffles

Makes twelve 4-inch square waffles

Golden and crunchy with cornmeal, and with a little tang from yogurt, these waffles are fantastic with traditional maple syrup, but try them with fruit-sweetened preserves for a delicious change.

Nonstick vegetable oil cooking spray, for waffle iron

1 cup unbleached all-purpose flour

½ cup yellow cornmeal, preferably stone-ground

1½ teaspoons baking powder

¼ teaspoon grated nutmeg

¼ teaspoon fine sea salt

¾ cup nonfat yogurt

⅓ cup canola oil

2 large eggs

¼ cup low-fat milk

2 tablespoons maple syrup

¼ teaspoon baking soda

⅓ cup hot water

1 Preheat a waffle iron. Lightly spray the waffle grids with vegetable oil spray. Preheat the oven to 200° F.

2 In a medium bowl, whisk the flour, cornmeal, baking powder, nutmeg, and salt to combine and make a well in the center.

3 In another medium bowl, whisk the yogurt, oil, eggs, milk, and maple syrup. Pour into the well and stir with a wooden spoon until almost smooth with a few lumps remaining. Dissolve the baking soda in ⅓ cup hot water, and stir gently into the batter.

4 Pour enough of the batter into the center of the waffle iron for it to come about 1 inch from the edges of the grid. Close the waffle iron and bake. The waffle will stop steaming from the sides when it is done. Remove the waffle from the iron, transfer to a baking sheet and keep warm in the oven while making the remaining waffles. Reheat the waffle iron again before proceeding. If the batter becomes thick upon standing, thin it with a little milk. Serve the waffles warm.

Apple Streusel Coffee Cake

Low Fat

Makes 12 servings

I love coffee cake, and it doesn't have to be fancy to get my attention. This one is plain and simple with apples and an oaty streusel topping. Baked in a shallow pan, the cake yields a lot of servings, so it's good to have on file for serving a crowd for brunch. Although it will be hard to resist nibbling at the coffee cake while it cools, let it cool completely before serving. Any gumminess in low-fat cakes is pronounced when they are warm.

COFFEE CAKE

Butter and all-purpose flour, for preparing pan

3 cups unbleached all-purpose flour

1½ teaspoons baking soda

1 teaspoon ground cinnamon

½ teaspoon ground ginger

¼ teaspoon ground allspice

½ teaspoon fine sea salt

1⅔ cups liquid fruit juice concentrate or Fruit Juice Reduction (page 23)

1¼ cups buttermilk

3 large eggs

1 medium tart cooking apple, such as Granny Smith, peeled, cored, and cut into ½-inch cubes

STREUSEL

½ cup maple sugar

⅓ cup rolled oats

⅓ cup chopped walnuts or pecans

3 tablespoons unsalted butter, softened

1 **To make the coffee cake:** Position a rack in the center of the oven and preheat to 350° F. Lightly butter and flour an 11 x 17 x 1-inch baking pan, tapping out excess flour.

2 Sift together the flour, baking soda, cinnamon, ginger, allspice, and salt into a medium bowl and make a well in the center.

3 In a small bowl, whisk together the fruit juice concentrate, buttermilk, and eggs until combined. Pour into the well and whisk just until combined. Do not overbeat. Stir in the apple. Transfer to the prepared pan and smooth the top.

4 **To make the streusel:** In a small bowl, work the maple sugar, oats, walnuts, and butter with your fingers until crumbly. Sprinkle evenly over the top of the batter.

5 Bake until a toothpick inserted in the center of the coffeecake comes out clean, 25 to 30 minutes. Cool completely in the pan on a wire cake rack. Cut into rectangles to serve.

Banana-Nut Pancakes

Dairy Free
Whole Grain

Makes 12 to 14 pancakes

Canola oil, for griddle

2 cups whole wheat pastry flour

1 teaspoon baking powder

¼ teaspoon baking soda

¼ teaspoon fine sea salt

1¼ cups plus 2 tablespoons soy milk

¾ cup mashed bananas (about 2 large very ripe bananas)

2 large eggs

3 tablespoons canola oil

½ cup (2 ounces) chopped pecans

Pancakes are a familiar sight on the breakfast table, but my favorites are these banana-and-nut-packed flapjacks. Serve them hot with genuine maple syrup—supermarket pancake syrup is nothing more than artificially flavored sugar syrup. While I have devised this as a dairy-free recipe, it works equally well with regular milk, so please try this recipe no matter what your lactose tolerance level.

1 Preheat a griddle or large skillet over medium heat until a sprinkle of water splashed on the surface immediately forms dancing droplets. Or preheat an electric frying pan to 350° F. Using a folded paper towel, lightly brush the griddle with oil. Preheat the oven to 200° F.

2 In a medium bowl, whisk the flour, baking powder, baking soda, and salt until combined and make a well in the center.

3 In another medium bowl, whisk all the soy milk, the bananas, eggs, and oil until well combined. Pour into the well and stir until smooth; there can be a few little lumps remaining. Stir in the pecans. Let stand for 5 minutes.

4 Using ¼ cup batter for each pancake, pour the batter onto the griddle. Cook until the edges of the pancake appear dry and the underside is golden brown, about 3 minutes. This pancake batter behaves differently from others: The top may not become covered with tiny bubbles, which usually indicate the pancake is ready to turn. Check the edges and use a pancake turner to peek at the underside. Flip the pancakes and cook until the other side is golden, about 2 minutes. Keep warm in the oven while preparing the rest of the pancakes. If the batter thickens too much upon standing, thin with additional soy milk. Serve warm.

About Scones

Scones are one of the best ways to start the day. Scones are made with a sticky dough that needs a little attention when mixing. A plastic bowl scraper, one of my favorite kitchen utensils, makes easy work out of this gooey job. It is shaped like a short, flat spade without the handle, curved at one end, conforming to a bowl's shape (to scrape out every last bit of recalcitrant dough), and straight at the opposite end (to scrape off those stubborn patches of dough that cling to your work surface after rolling out or kneading.) Holding the scraper at the curved end, use the straight edge as a kind of spoon while mixing the scone dough, cutting through the dough while mixing. This works much better than simply stirring, as the dough sticks constantly to the spoon and needs to be scraped off after a couple of stirs. The straight edge of a metal or plastic pancake turner-type of spatula works well, too. Inexpensive and versatile plastic dough scrapers can be found in some kitchenware shops, but are most easily available at professional bakery supply stores. (I get mine from wholesale grocery suppliers, who have them stamped with their names as promotional gifts.)

Banana-Pecan Scones

Egg Free

Makes 8 scones

These scones are full of bananas (two cups of sliced bananas for only eight scones!), making for a moist dough that must be baked thoroughly to avoid any gumminess. Be sure to use well-ripened bananas, or your scones just won't be banana-y enough. Also, take the time to toast the pecans; that minor step adds major flavor.

All-purpose flour, for the baking sheet

¾ cup (3 ounces) pecans

2¼ cups unbleached all-purpose flour, plus more if needed

2 teaspoons baking powder

½ teaspoon ground cinnamon

¼ teaspoon ground ginger

¼ teaspoon fine sea salt

4 tablespoons (½ stick) unsalted butter, chilled, cut into ½-inch pieces

½ cup liquid fruit juice concentrate or Fruit Juice Reduction (page 23)

⅓ cup milk

4 well-ripened medium bananas, cut into ⅓-inch slices (2 cups)

Milk, for glazing

1 Position a rack in the top third of the oven and preheat the oven to 350° F. Sprinkle a baking sheet generously with flour and set aside.

2 Spread the pecans in a single layer on an unfloured baking sheet. Bake, stirring often, until lightly toasted and fragrant, about 10 minutes. Cool the pecans completely, then coarsely chop.

3 Increase the oven temperature to 400° F. Sift together the flour, baking powder, cinnamon, ginger, and salt into a medium bowl. Add the butter. Using a pastry blender or 2 forks, cut the butter into the flour until the mixture resembles coarse meal. Make a well in the center.

4 In a small bowl, whisk together the fruit juice concentrate and milk until combined. Pour half the liquid ingredients into the well. Add the bananas and pecans. Using a plastic dough divider or the edge of a metal spatula, turn and cut the dough, gradually adding the remaining liquid, until the bananas are chopped and the mixture comes together into a soft, slightly sticky dough. Using floured hands, gently knead the dough in the bowl to form a ball. Add a tablespoon or two of additional flour, if necessary, but remember the dough should be slightly sticky.

5 Transfer the dough to the floured baking sheet. Pat out the dough to make a 9-inch circle about ½ inch thick. Be sure there is enough flour under the dough to prevent sticking. Using a sharp knife, cut the dough into 8 equal wedges, but do not separate the wedges. Brush the top with a little milk to glaze.

6 Bake until the edges are beginning to brown, about 10 minutes. Reduce the heat to 350° F. and continue baking until the top is lightly browned and the area where the points of the scones converge looks quite dry, about 15 minutes. Cool the scones on the baking sheet for at least 10 minutes. Break apart and serve warm.

Cranberry-Walnut Scones

Egg Free

Makes 8 scones

Scones are indispensable at teatime in Britain. We serve a lot of them in the afternoon at Mäni's, but people seem to love them for breakfast even more. These particular scones are chunky with cranberries and nuts—you could use dried cranberries or even raisins as an alternative if you want to make these when fresh cranberries are out of season.

All-purpose flour, for the baking sheet

1¾ cup unbleached all-purpose flour, plus more if needed

2 teaspoons baking powder

¼ teaspoon ground cinnamon

4 tablespoons (½ stick) unsalted butter, chilled, cut into ½-inch pieces

½ cup liquid fruit juice concentrate or Fruit Juice Reduction (page 23)

⅓ cup milk

Grated zest of 1 orange

½ cup fresh or frozen cranberries

½ cup (2 ounces) chopped walnuts

Milk, for glazing

1 Position a rack in the center of the oven and preheat the oven to 400° F. Sprinkle a baking sheet generously with flour.

2 Sift together the flour, baking powder and cinnamon into a medium bowl. Add the butter. Using a pastry blender or 2 forks, cut the butter into the flour until the mixture resembles coarse meal. Make a well in the center of the mixture.

3 In a small bowl, whisk the fruit juice concentrate, milk, and orange zest until combined. Pour half the liquid into the well. Add the cranberries and walnuts. Using a plastic dough divider or the edge of a metal spatula, turn and cut the dough, gradually adding the remaining liquid, until the mixture comes together into a soft, sticky dough. Using floured hands, gently knead the dough in the bowl to form a ball. Add a tablespoon or two of additional flour, if necessary, but remember the dough should be slightly sticky.

4 Transfer to the baking sheet. Pat out the dough to make a 9-inch circle about ½ inch thick. Be sure there is enough flour under the dough to prevent sticking. Using a sharp knife, cut the dough into 8 equal wedges, but do not separate the wedges. Brush the top with a little milk to glaze.

5 Bake until the edges of the scones are lightly browned, about 15 minutes. Cool on the pan for at least 10 minutes. Break apart and serve warm.

Fresh Strawberry Scones

Egg Free
Low Fat

These are a variation on my basic scone recipe with a surprise filling of fresh berries. They are at their best when served warm from the oven, perhaps with a pat of butter melted on top.

Makes 8 scones

1¾ cups unbleached all-purpose flour, plus more if needed

2 teaspoons baking powder

¼ teaspoon fine sea salt

4 tablespoons (½ stick) unsalted butter, chilled, cut into bits

½ cup liquid fruit juice concentrate or Fruit Juice Reduction (page 23)

⅓ cup milk

Grated zest of 1 lemon

All-purpose flour, for the baking sheet

2 cups sliced strawberries

4 tablespoons fruit-sweetened strawberry spread

Milk, for glazing

1 Sift together the flour, baking powder, and salt into a medium bowl. Add the butter. Using a pastry blender or 2 forks, cut the butter into the flour until the mixture resembles coarse meal. Make a well in the center of the mixture.

2 In a small bowl, whisk the fruit juice concentrate, milk, and lemon zest until combined. Pour half the liquid into the well. Using a plastic dough divider or the edge of a metal spatula, turn and cut the dough, gradually adding the remaining liquid, until the mixture comes together into a soft, slightly sticky dough. Using floured hands, gently knead the dough in the bowl to form a ball. Add a tablespoon or two of additional flour, if necessary, but remember the dough should be slightly sticky. On a lightly floured work surface, pat the dough into a thick disk about 9 inches in diameter and ¾ inch thick, and wrap completely in plastic wrap.

Refrigerate until the dough is firm enough to slice horizontally, at least 1 hour or up to 4 hours.

3 Position a rack in the center of the oven and preheat to 400° F. Generously sprinkle a baking sheet with flour.

4 Using a serrated knife, cut the dough horizontally into 2 pieces. Transfer the top half of the dough to the prepared baking sheet. You may find it helpful to slip a thin rimless baking sheet or the bottom of a tart pan under the dough to help. Arrange the strawberries over the dough. Drop the strawberry spread over the berries in heaping teaspoon-size dollops, leaving a 1-inch border around the edge of the dough. Place the remaining dough disk over the berries. Crimp the edges of the dough circles together. Be sure there is enough flour under the dough to prevent sticking. Using a sharp knife, cut the dough into 8 equal wedges but do not separate the wedges. Brush the top lightly with milk to glaze.

5 Bake until the edges of the scones are lightly browned, 15 to 20 minutes. Cool on the pan for at least 10 minutes. Cut the scones apart and serve warm.

Barley-Currant Scones

Dairy Free
Wheat Free

Makes 16 scones

Barley flour makes a surprisingly tender scone with a wonderful whole-grain flavor. This version makes individual, biscuitlike rounds, rather than the more traditional wedge shape. The barley-based dough bakes more evenly this way. Be sure to sift the barley flour to avoid a heavy dough.

Nonstick vegetable oil cooking spray, for the pan

4¼ cups barley flour

1½ teaspoons baking soda

½ teaspoon ground cinnamon

½ teaspoon grated nutmeg

½ teaspoon fine sea salt

¾ cup liquid fruit juice concentrate or Fruit Juice Reduction (page 23)

½ cup canola oil

2 large eggs

¼ cup soy milk

Grated zest of 1 orange

1 cup dried currants

1 egg yolk mixed with 1 tablespoon milk, for glaze

1 Position a rack in the center of the oven and preheat the oven to 375° F. Lightly spray a large baking sheet with vegetable oil spray.

2 Sift together the barley flour, baking soda, cinnamon, nutmeg, and salt into a medium bowl and make a well in the center.

3 In a medium bowl, using a handheld electric mixer set at medium speed, beat the fruit juice concentrate, oil, eggs, soy milk, and orange zest until very foamy, about 1 minute. Pour into the well and stir with a wooden spoon to form a soft dough. Stir in the currants.

4 Using floured hands, turn out the dough onto a lightly floured work surface (you may use either barley or unbleached flour). Pat out the dough until ½ inch thick. Using a 3-inch round fluted biscuit cutter, cut out scones and transfer to the prepared baking sheet. Gather up the scraps and knead together briefly. Pat out again and cut out more scones. Repeat until all of the dough has been used. Brush the tops of the scones lightly with the egg yolk glaze.

5 Bake until the tops of the scones are golden brown and spring back when pressed lightly in the center with a finger, 12 to 15 minutes. Cool slightly on a wire cake rack and serve warm.

Mäni's Muffins

Muffin madness has hit America. Muffins are like having your own little cake on a plate, and you can eat it any way you want to—a tiny nibble at a time, in big bites, or even with a fork.

Muffins can be enjoyed at any time of day, as a quick breakfast, in the lunchbox, as an afternoon pick-me-up, or as dessert. Bakers love to make them because they are easy, bake up in short order, and don't need to be frosted. They are at their best hot out of the oven for instant gratification, but I haven't known too many people who turn down cooled muffins, either. I find that they are one of the best opportunities for the reduced-fat treatment, so I always have a lot of them on the menu at the bakery for those muffin lovers who must have theirs every morning.

As simple as muffins are, I have a few tips to help you bake perfect muffins every time.

❧ These recipes were designed for standard muffin cups, 2½ inches wide and 1½ inches deep. You can experiment with other sizes, such as the jumbo Texas or mini-muffin tins, increasing or decreasing the cooking times and testing for doneness according to the recipe.

❧ Not all of these muffin recipes make an even dozen. When reducing the batch size for this book's recipes down from my large-scale bakery recipes, I used the adapted recipe when it was at its best, even if it yielded an untraditional number of muffins.

Peach–Poppy Seed, Chocolate-Walnut, Carrot-Pineapple, Raspberry-Oat Flour, and Raisin Bran Muffins

If you wish, add about one and a half tablespoons of water to each empty muffin cup in the pan to act as a precaution against uneven baking. I practically never have a full muffin pan at the bakery and haven't had this problem, but home ovens often have more quirks than professional ones. The water will act as an insulator. Be careful not to splash the water into the batter in the cups.

Use a nonstick muffin pan, so if your muffins rise over the top the batter won't stick to the top surface of the pan. To be extra sure that the muffins won't stick, spray the pan with nonstick vegetable oil cooking spray.

Use paper baking liners (the kind used for cupcakes) only when specified in the recipe. Some of these batters will stick even to nonstick surfaces, so the paper liners are important. Conversely, some batters stick to the paper liners and make them difficult to peel off; these are better baked in unlined pans. Simply follow the instructions in the recipe.

Be careful not to overmix muffins. Mixing activates the gluten in wheat flour and makes the muffins tough. Stir just until the batter is barely smooth. If you are stirring in raisins or other additions, stop stirring when there are still a few lumps, then add the raisins and mix until smooth.

Fill the muffin cups a little more than three-fourths full so the muffins rise to their familiar domed shape.

Let the muffins cool for a few minutes before running a knife around the edges and unmolding. It's hard to wait, but the muffins will fall apart if you try to remove them from the pan too soon. However, they are at their best when eaten the day they are made.

Blueberry Corn Muffins

Makes 8 muffins

If I had to pick a favorite grain, I would probably choose corn. Blueberries make a delightful addition to familiar corn muffins. Place paper liners in the muffin cups, as the natural sugars found in cornmeal make this a batter that can stick easily to the pan.

Paper muffin liners, for pan

1 cup yellow cornmeal, preferably stone-ground

1 cup unbleached all-purpose flour

1 teaspoon baking soda

¾ teaspoon baking powder

¼ teaspoon fine sea salt

1 cup buttermilk

¼ cup plus 2 tablespoons liquid fruit juice concentrate or Fruit Juice Reduction (page 23)

¼ cup canola oil

1 large egg

1 cup fresh or frozen blueberries

1 Position a rack in the center of the oven and preheat the oven to 350° F. Line 8 standard muffin cups with paper muffin liners.

2 In a medium bowl, whisk the cornmeal, flour, baking soda, baking powder, and salt to combine and make a well in the center.

3 In another medium bowl, whisk the buttermilk, all the fruit juice concentrate, the oil, and egg until frothy. Pour into the well and stir with a wooden spoon just until combined. Fold in the blueberries. Do not overmix.

4 Spoon the batter into the muffin cups, filling almost completely full. Bake until the tops are golden brown and a toothpick inserted in the center of a muffin comes out clean, 20 to 25 minutes. Remove from the cups. Serve the muffins warm or at room temperature.

Chocolate-Walnut Muffins

Egg Free
Dairy Free
Whole Grain

Makes 9 muffins

These muffins are deep, dark, and chocolaty and are truly amazing when one considers what they don't have in them. The crunchy walnut-maple topping is a nice touch.

Nonstick vegetable oil cooking spray, for preparing the pan

1¼ cups whole wheat pastry flour

½ cup cocoa powder (not Dutch processed)

½ teaspoon baking soda

½ teaspoon baking powder

½ teaspoon fine sea salt

½ cup liquid fruit juice concentrate or Fruit Juice Reduction (page 23)

¾ cup soy milk

3 tablespoons canola oil

½ cup (2 ounces) chopped walnuts, divided

2 teaspoons maple sugar

1 Position a rack in the center of the oven and preheat the oven to 350° F. Lightly spray a standard muffin pan with vegetable oil spray.

2 Sift the flour, cocoa, baking soda, baking powder, and salt into a medium bowl and make a well in the center.

3 In another medium bowl, whisk the fruit juice concentrate, soy milk, and oil until frothy. Pour into the well and stir with a wooden spoon just until combined. Fold in ⅓ cup of the chopped walnuts. Do not overbeat.

4 In a small bowl, combine the *remaining* walnuts with the maple sugar. Divide the batter among 9 muffin cups, filling each cup almost completely full. Sprinkle the tops of the muffins with the walnut–maple sugar mixture. Bake the muffins until a toothpick inserted in the centers comes out clean and the tops spring back when pressed with a finger, 18 to 20 minutes. Cool for 2 minutes, run a knife around the inside of the cups to release the muffins, and remove from the cups. Serve the muffins warm or at room temperature.

Oil-Free Cornmeal Muffins

No Added Fat

Makes 8 muffins

Cornbread purists, myself included, may question the taste of a no-fat-added cornmeal muffin. But my experimentation paid off, creating a wonderful grainy but not heavy muffin without the excessive butter or oil often found in other versions. Enjoy the muffins warm out of the oven, slathered with your favorite fruit-sweetened spread.

Nonstick vegetable oil cooking spray, for pan

1½ cups unbleached all-purpose flour

½ cup yellow cornmeal, preferably stone-ground

2 tablespoons maple sugar

¾ teaspoon baking soda

¼ teaspoon fine sea salt

½ cup liquid fruit juice concentrate or Fruit Juice Reduction (page 23)

½ cup buttermilk

2 large eggs

Grated zest of 1 lemon (optional)

1 Position a rack in the center of the oven and preheat the oven to 350° F. Lightly spray the insides of 8 standard muffin cups, preferably nonstick, with vegetable oil spray.

2 In a medium bowl, whisk the flour, cornmeal, maple sugar, baking soda, and salt and make a well in the center.

3 In another medium bowl, whisk the fruit juice concentrate, buttermilk, eggs, and lemon zest, if using. Pour into the well and stir with a wooden spoon just until combined.

4 Spoon the batter evenly into 8 of the muffin cups. Bake until the tops spring back when pressed lightly, about 18 minutes. Cool for 2 minutes, run a knife around the inside of the cups to release the muffins, and remove from the cups. Serve the muffins warm or at room temperature.

Blueberry–Oat Bran Muffins

Egg Free
Dairy Free
Whole Grain

Blueberry is the best-selling kind of muffin in the United States. Here's a version for everybody, including people who have to avoid dairy products and eggs.

Makes 12 muffins

Nonstick vegetable oil cooking spray, for pan

1¼ cups whole wheat pastry flour

½ cup oat bran

½ teaspoon baking soda

½ teaspoon baking powder

¼ teaspoon fine sea salt

¾ cup soy milk

⅓ cup liquid fruit juice concentrate or Fruit Juice Reduction (page 23)

3 tablespoons canola oil

1 cup fresh or frozen blueberries

1 Position a rack in the center of the oven and preheat the oven to 350° F. Lightly spray a standard muffin pan with vegetable oil spray.

2 In a medium bowl, whisk the flour, oat bran, baking soda, baking powder, and salt to combine and make a well in the center.

3 In another medium bowl, whisk the soy milk, fruit juice concentrate, and oil until the surface is bubbly. Pour into the well and stir with a wooden spoon just until smooth. Stir in the blueberries. (The batter will seem a little more liquid than usual.)

4 Divide the batter evenly among the muffin cups. Bake until a toothpick inserted in the center of a muffin comes out clean and the top springs back when pressed lightly, about 20 minutes. Cool for 2 minutes, run a knife around the inside of the cups to release the muffins, and remove from the cups. Serve the muffins warm or at room temperature.

Huckleberry-Apple Muffins

Makes about 10 muffins

This is one of my absolutely favorite muffins, not just because my grandparents' cabin in my home state of Idaho is surrounded by huckleberry bushes. If you aren't fortunate enough to have a huckleberry patch nearby—or you aren't up to the job of gathering enough of the tiny berries—feel free to use blueberries or raspberries.

Paper muffin liners, for the pan

2 cups plus 1 tablespoon unbleached all-purpose flour, divided

½ teaspoon baking soda

½ teaspoon baking powder

¼ teaspoon fine sea salt

1 cup liquid fruit juice concentrate or Fruit Juice Reduction (page 23)

1 cup milk

2 large eggs

6 tablespoons unsalted butter, melted

Grated zest of 1 lemon

1 cup fresh huckleberries or blueberries

1 medium tart cooking apple, such as Granny Smith, peeled, cored, and cut into ¼-inch dice

1 Position a rack in the center of the oven and preheat the oven to 350° F. Line 10 standard muffin cups with paper muffin liners.

2 Sift *2 cups* of the flour, baking soda, baking powder, and salt together into a medium bowl and make a well in the center.

3 In another medium bowl, whisk the fruit juice concentrate, milk, eggs, butter, and lemon zest. Pour into the well and stir with a wooden spoon just until smooth. In a small bowl, toss the huckleberries with the *remaining 1 tablespoon* flour. Add to the batter along with the apples and stir in. Do not overmix.

4 Spoon the batter into the muffin cups, filling almost completely full. Bake until the tops are golden brown and a toothpick inserted in the center of a muffin comes out clean, about 25 minutes. Remove from the cups. Serve the muffins warm or at room temperature.

Washington State Blackberry Muffins

Makes 10 muffins

Washington is known for its plump, sweet-tart wild blackberries. In August, whether in a forest or park, on oceanside cliffs, along a country road, or out in the backyard, you can barely walk without running into jumbles of dark, juicy berries. They are so big it won't take long to pick enough for this recipe, and they freeze so well you can make these muffins all year long. Place them in a single layer on a baking sheet and freeze, uncovered, until hard, then transfer to airtight zipper-locked bags to store in the freezer.

Nonstick vegetable oil cooking spray, for pan

1½ cups plus 1 tablespoon unbleached all-purpose flour, divided

½ teaspoon baking soda

½ teaspoon baking powder

¼ teaspoon fine sea salt

½ cup milk

½ cup liquid fruit juice concentrate or Fruit Juice Reduction (page 23)

3 tablespoons unsalted butter, melted

1 large egg

Grated zest of 1 lemon

1½ cups fresh or frozen blackberries

1 Position a rack in the center of the oven and preheat the oven to 350° F. Lightly spray a standard muffin pan with vegetable oil spray.

2 In a medium bowl, whisk *1½ cups* of the flour, the baking soda, baking powder, and salt until combined and make a well in the center.

3 In a medium bowl, whisk the milk, fruit juice concentrate, butter, egg, and lemon zest until combined. Pour into the well and stir with a wooden spoon just until smooth. In a small bowl, toss the blackberries with the *remaining 1 tablespoon* flour. Add the berries to the batter and fold in gently. Do not overmix.

4 Spoon the batter into 10 of the muffin cups, filling each cup almost completely full. Bake the muffins until a toothpick inserted in the centers comes out clean and the tops spring back when pressed with a finger, about 20 minutes. Cool for 2 minutes, run a knife around the inside of the cups to release the muffins, and remove from the cups. Serve the muffins warm or at room temperature.

Raspberry–Oat Flour Muffins

Wheat Free

Makes 12 muffins

Raspberries and lemons combine to add a sweet-tart edge to these wheatless muffins. Paper muffin liners are imperative—the batter will stick even to nonstick muffin cups.

Paper muffin liners, for pan

6 tablespoons unsalted butter, at room temperature

⅔ cup liquid fruit juice concentrate or Fruit Juice Reduction (page 23)

2 large eggs, at room temperature

Grated zest of 1 lemon

2 tablespoons fresh lemon juice

2 cups plus 2 tablespoons oat flour

1¼ teaspoons baking soda

1 cup fresh or frozen raspberries

1 Position a rack in the center of the oven and preheat the oven to 350° F. Line 12 standard muffin cups with paper muffin liners.

2 In a medium bowl, using a handheld electric mixer set at medium speed, beat the butter until creamy, about 1 minute. Gradually beat in the fruit juice concentrate. Beat in the eggs, one at a time, beating well after each addition. Beat in the lemon zest and lemon juice.

3 Sift together all the oat flour and the baking soda into a medium bowl. Add to the butter mixture and beat just until smooth. Stir in the raspberries.

4 Divide the batter evenly among the muffin cups. Bake until a toothpick inserted in the centers comes out clean and the tops spring back when pressed lightly, about 20 minutes. Cool for 5 minutes before removing from the pan. Serve the muffins warm or at room temperature.

Banana-Walnut Muffins

Whole Grain

Makes 10 muffins

Use quite ripe bananas for this recipe, the riper the better! They should be well-covered with brown spots, or even black, but shouldn't have a sharp, alcoholic odor. Your muffins will only be as good as your bananas. I personally can't imagine that sweet taste of banana without a toasted, nutty crunch to follow. Use paper muffin liners to avoid having the muffins stick to the pan.

Paper muffin liners, for pan

1¾ cups whole wheat pastry flour

½ cup oat bran

1 teaspoon baking soda

1 teaspoon ground cinnamon

½ teaspoon fine sea salt

¼ teaspoon ground ginger

¾ cup plus 2 tablespoons liquid fruit juice concentrate or Fruit Juice Reduction (page 23)

⅔ cup mashed ripe bananas (about 2 medium bananas)

¼ cup low-fat milk

1 large egg

1 large egg white

2 tablespoons canola oil

½ cup coarsely chopped walnuts

10 walnut halves, for topping

1 Position a rack in the center of the oven and preheat the oven to 350° F. Line 10 standard muffin cups with paper muffin liners.

2 In a medium bowl, whisk the flour, bran, baking soda, cinnamon, salt, and ginger to mix and make a well in the center.

3 In another medium bowl, using a handheld electric mixer set at medium speed, beat all the fruit juice concentrate, the banana puree, milk, egg, egg white, and oil until well mixed and frothy, about 1 minute. Pour into the well. Reduce the speed to low and mix just until combined. Do not overbeat. Stir in the walnuts.

4 Spoon the batter into the muffin cups, filling each almost completely full. Top each muffin with a walnut half. Bake the muffins until a toothpick inserted in the centers comes out clean and the tops spring back when pressed with a finger, about 20 minutes. Cool for 2 minutes, then remove from the cups. Cool on a wire cake rack. Serve the muffins warm or at room temperature.

Raisin Bran Muffins

Low Fat
Egg Free
Whole Grain

Makes about 10 muffins

Raisin bran muffins are a morning classic. For superlative muffins, get raisins at a natural foods store. Try the plump Monuka variety.

Paper muffin liners, for pan

1¼ cups whole wheat pastry flour

½ cup wheat bran

½ teaspoon baking soda

½ teaspoon baking powder

¼ teaspoon fine sea salt

¾ cup skim milk

⅓ cup liquid fruit juice concentrate or Fruit Juice Reduction (page 23)

2½ tablespoons canola oil

1 cup raisins

1 Position a rack in the center of the oven and preheat the oven to 350° F. Line 10 standard muffin cups with paper muffin liners.

2 In a medium bowl, whisk the flour, bran, baking soda, baking powder, and salt to combine and make a well in the center.

3 In another medium bowl, whisk the milk, fruit juice concentrate, and oil until frothy. Pour into the well and stir with a wooden spoon just until combined. Fold in the raisins. Do not overbeat.

4 Spoon the batter into 10 of the muffin cups, filling each cup almost completely full. Bake until a toothpick inserted in the centers comes out clean and the tops spring back when pressed with a finger, 20 to 25 minutes. Cool for 2 minutes, run a knife around the inside of the cups to release the muffins, and remove from the cups. Serve warm or at room temperature.

The Cookie Jar

Cookies come in all shapes and sizes, flavors and textures. All of these possibilities add to their appeal. From the romantically shaped Chocolate Truffle Hearts to the homespun Chocolate Chip and Pecan Cookies, from the almost austere Almond Shortbread to decadent Deep Dark Brownies, there's a cookie here for everyone.

Even the best cookie dough can run into trouble during the baking process. The biggest villain is thin, poorly insulated cookie sheets, which can allow the cookies to burn. To avoid blackened cookie bottoms, use heavy, shiny cookie sheets that have not darkened with age and use.

One of the saddest things that can happen to a baker is to have the cookies stick to the pan. I recommend that you line your baking sheets with nonstick parchment paper. Lining with parchment paper not only keeps the cookies from sticking, it also helps cleaning up, as the paper can be changed without washing the sheet. Most of these cookies can be made on baking sheets sprayed with nonstick spray, but in recipes where I specify using parchment paper instead of spraying the baking sheet, do use the parchment paper because that particular dough may stick even to nonstick surfaces. Parchment paper is available at most kitchenware shops and many supermarkets, but if you go to a restaurant or bakery supply house, you can economically buy a large box that will last forever. In fact, it may be so much that you can share it with friends who love to bake.

Chocolate-dipped Barley Cookies, Chocolate Chip and Pecan Cookies, Red Hot Peanut Butter Cookies

You will find a few low-fat cookie recipes in this chapter. As with all low-fat doughs, it is very important not to overmix the batter, or cookies may be tough. Bake low-fat cookies only until the edges are lightly browned and the tops of the cookies spring back when lightly pressed with a finger. If the cookies are baked until the the tops are browned, they may dry out when cooled. Many of the cookies use maple sugar, which helps achieve the traditional range of cookie textures. Cookies sweetened entirely with liquid fruit juice concentrate will be moist and chewy due to the concentrate's high moisture content.

I have been specific about where to place the oven racks in the oven. Cookies baked in the top third will brown faster. I also remind you to switch the position of the baking sheets from top to bottom halfway through the baking to ensure even browning.

Chocolate Chip and Pecan Cookies

Egg Free
Dairy Free
Whole Grain

Makes about 18 cookies

Rich and bursting with real chocolate flavor, just like a Toll House cookie. This recipe proves that you can make a tasty cookie without eggs or dairy products. Don't be surprised if the chocolate chips around the edges of the cookie melt. This is because malt-sweetened chocolate chips don't have as much of the emulsifying ingredient lecithin as supermarket chips. If this bothers you, simply flake off the excess chips after baking. For a special treat, dip the cookies after baking as described on page 64.

Nonstick vegetable oil cooking spray, for the baking sheets

6 tablespoons (¾ stick) safflower oil margarine or butter, at room temperature

1 cup liquid fruit juice concentrate or Fruit Juice Reduction (page 23)

2 teaspoons vanilla extract

1¾ cups plus 2 tablespoons whole wheat pastry flour

½ teaspoon baking soda

½ teaspoon fine sea salt

1 cup (6 ounces) malt-sweetened semisweet chocolate chips

¾ cup (3 ounces) pecans, chopped

1 Position racks in the center and top third of the oven and preheat the oven to 350° F. Lightly spray 2 large baking sheets with vegetable oil spray.

2 In a medium bowl, using a handheld electric mixer set at medium speed, beat the margarine until creamy, about 1 minute. Add the fruit juice concentrate and vanilla and beat until mixed.

3 In a medium bowl, whisk all the flour, the baking soda, and salt to mix. Add to the margarine and stir with a wooden spoon to make a soft dough. Stir in the chocolate chips and pecans. Using a heaping tablespoon for each cookie, drop the dough about 2 inches apart onto the baking sheets.

4 Bake the cookies until the edges are lightly browned, about 15 minutes. Halfway through baking, switch the position of the sheets from top to bottom. Cool for 2 minutes on the baking sheets, then transfer to wire cake racks to cool completely.

Deep Dark Brownies

Makes 16 brownies

While a lot of fat-free and reduced-fat brownies are flooding the market, let's take a look at the building blocks of this American classic: chocolate, butter, eggs, and nuts. Where does one begin to cut the fat yet retain the rich and creamy, chewy chocolate denseness that is the very definition of a brownie? My answer is, don't even try!

Butter and all-purpose flour, for the pan

12 tablespoons (1½ sticks) unsalted butter

2 cups (12 ounces) malt-sweetened semisweet chocolate chips

1 cup liquid fruit juice concentrate or Fruit Juice Reduction (page 23)

⅓ cup maple sugar

3 large eggs, at room temperature

1 tablespoon vanilla extract

1 cup unbleached all-purpose flour

½ teaspoon fine sea salt

1 cup (4 ounces) walnuts, coarsely chopped

1 Position a rack in the center of the oven and preheat the oven to 350° F. Lightly butter and flour a 9 x13-inch baking pan, tapping out excess flour.

2 In a medium saucepan, melt the butter over medium heat. Remove from heat and add the chocolate chips. Let stand until the chips are softened, about 3 minutes. Whisk until smooth. Let stand until tepid, about 10 minutes.

3 Whisk in the fruit juice concentrate and maple sugar. Whisk in the eggs, one at a time, then the vanilla. Add the flour and salt and whisk just until smooth. Stir in the walnuts. Spread evenly in the baking pan.

4 Bake until a toothpick inserted 2 inches from the edge of the pan comes out clean, about 25 minutes. Do not overbake. Cool completely on a wire cake rack.

Chocolate-dipped Barley Cookies

Egg Free
Dairy Free
Wheat Free

Makes about 18 cookies

A dip in melted chocolate adds another dimension to these wheat-free cookies which, while tender and tasty, would be a little too plain on their own.

COOKIES

Nonstick vegetable oil cooking spray, for the baking sheets

2 cups barley flour

½ teaspoon baking soda

¼ teaspoon fine sea salt

¾ cup fruit juice concentrate or Fruit Juice Reduction (page 23)

6 tablespoons canola oil

CHOCOLATE FOR DIPPING

1 cup (6 ounces) malt-sweetened semisweet chocolate chips

1 teaspoon vegetable oil

1 Position racks in the top third and center of the oven and preheat the oven to 350° F. Lightly spray 2 baking sheets with vegetable oil spray.

2 **To make the cookies:** Sift the barley flour, baking soda, and salt into a medium bowl and make a well in the center.

3 In a small bowl, whisk the fruit juice concentrate and all the oil until combined. Pour into the well and mix with a wooden spoon to form a sticky dough. Transfer the dough to a pastry bag fitted with a large open star tip, such as Ateco Number 5. Holding the tip about ½ inch above the baking sheet, press out 2-inch-wide stars of dough, spacing them about 1 inch apart, as the cookies will spread a little during baking.

4 Bake until the edges of the cookies are lightly browned, 12 to 15 minutes. Transfer the cookies to a wire cake rack to cool completely.

5 **To dip the cookies:** In a heatproof medium bowl set over hot, not simmering, water, melt the chocolate and oil, stirring occasionally until smooth. Tilt the bowl in the double boiler so the chocolate collects in a deep pool. Line a clean baking sheet with parchment or wax paper. Hold a cookie by the edge and quickly dip halfway into the melted chocolate. Remove the cookie, shaking to remove excess chocolate. Drag the bottom of the cookie along the lip of the bowl to remove more excess chocolate. Place the cookie on the baking sheet. Refrigerate to set the chocolate, about 15 minutes. Store the cookies at room temperature in an airtight container with wax paper separating the layers.

Granola Triple Oat Cookies

Egg Free
Dairy Free
Wheat Free
Whole Grain

Makes about 18 cookies

With not just the rolled oats every oatmeal cookie has, but oat flour and even oat bran, these cookies are full of fiber and flavor. It is amazingly light for a whole-grain, wheatless cookie, and one of my personal favorites.

Parchment paper, for the baking sheets

2¼ cups oat flour

½ teaspoon baking soda

½ teaspoon ground cinnamon

¼ teaspoon fine sea salt

¼ cup oat bran

¼ cup rolled old-fashioned oats

¾ cup plus 2 tablespoons liquid fruit juice concentrate or Fruit Juice Reduction (page 23)

6 tablespoons canola oil

1½ teaspoons vanilla

½ cup raisins

½ cup (2 ounces) walnuts, chopped

1 Position racks in the center and top third of the oven and preheat the oven to 350° F. Line 2 large baking sheets with parchment paper.

2 Sift the oat flour, baking soda, cinnamon, and salt into a medium bowl. Add the oat bran and rolled oats and whisk to combine. Make a well in the center.

3 In another medium bowl, whisk all the fruit juice concentrate, the oil, and the vanilla until combined. Pour into the well and mix with a wooden spoon. Stir in the raisins and walnuts. Cover and refrigerate until firm enough to scoop, about 1 hour.

4 Using about 3 tablespoons for each cookie (scantly filling a ¼-cup measuring cup works well), transfer the dough to the baking sheets, spacing about 2 inches apart. Bake the cookies until the edges are lightly browned and they feel firm in the center when pressed with a finger, 10 to 12 minutes. Halfway through baking, switch the positions of the baking sheets from top to bottom. Cool the cookies for 2 minutes on the baking sheets, then transfer to a wire cake rack to cool completely.

Chocolate Truffle Heart Cookies

Makes about 16 large cookies

The unofficial name for this cookie is the Marewich, in honor of my friend Mary Coller, at whose request it came to be. Big and heart shaped, it has a melt-in-your-mouth chocolate truffle filling sandwiched between two cookie layers. As the cookie dough must be well chilled before rolling out and the truffle cream takes some time to cool and thicken, I suggest starting these components the day before. Also, the cookies need to be refrigerated for at least an hour before serving. The humidity in the refrigerator firms the filling and adds a chewiness to the cookies that can't be achieved in any other fashion.

COOKIES

10 tablespoons (1¼ sticks) unsalted butter, at room temperature

¾ cup maple sugar

½ cup liquid fruit juice concentrate or Fruit Juice Reduction (page 23)

1 large egg

2½ cups unbleached all-purpose flour

1 teaspoon baking soda

¼ teaspoon fine sea salt

TRUFFLE CREAM

⅔ cup heavy (whipping) cream

2 cups (12 ounces) malt-sweetened semisweet chocolate chips

Nonstick vegetable oil cooking spray, for baking sheets

1 **To make the cookies:** In a medium bowl, using a handheld electric mixer set at medium speed, beat the butter until creamy, about 1 minute. Add the maple sugar, fruit juice concentrate, and egg and beat until lighter in color, about 2 minutes.

2 Sift together the flour, baking soda, and salt. Add to the butter mixture and stir with a wooden spoon to make a soft dough. Transfer to a large piece of plastic wrap and form into a thick disk. Wrap in the plastic and refrigerate until well chilled, at least 4 hours or overnight.

3 **To make the truffle cream:** In a small saucepan over low heat, cook the cream just until small bubbles appear around the edges. Place the chocolate chips in a small bowl. Pour the hot cream over the chocolate chips and let stand until the chips are softened, about 5 minutes. Whisk until smooth. Let stand until cooled to room temperature and thick enough to spread, about 4 hours. (The cooling can be hastened by placing the bowl in a larger bowl of iced water. Let stand, stirring occasionally, until the cream is cooled and thickened but not chilled and hardened.) Do not refrigerate.

4 **To assemble:** Position racks in the top third and center of the oven and preheat the oven to 375° F. Lightly spray 2 baking sheets with vegetable oil spray.

5 Remove half of the dough from the refrigerator, keeping the remaining dough chilled. Cover with plastic wrap and let stand until slightly softened and easier to roll out, about 5 minutes. On a lightly floured work surface, roll out the dough about ¼ inch thick. If the dough cracks, it is too cold; let it stand for a few minutes before trying again. Using a 3½-inch-wide heart-shape cookie cutter, cut out the cookies and transfer to the baking sheet, placing the cookies about 1 ½ inches apart. Gather up the scraps, place in a plastic bag, and refrigerate. Bake the cookies until golden brown, 8 to 10 minutes. Halfway through baking, switch the positions of the sheets from top to bottom. Transfer to a wire cake rack to cool completely. Repeat the procedure with the half portion of dough to bake a second batch of cookies. Make sure that the baking sheets are completely cooled before respraying them and baking the next batch. Add the scraps to the ones already in the refrigerator. To make a final batch of cookies, knead the scraps together and repeat the procedure.

6 Using a heaping tablespoon of truffle cream for each, sandwich 2 cookie hearts, flat sides facing in. Press gently so the filling spreads out. Place on a baking sheet and cover with plastic wrap. Refrigerate for at least 1 hour before serving. These cookies should be stored and served cold.

Applesauce-Currant Cookies

Low Fat
Dairy Free
Whole Grain

Makes about 24 cookies

These cookies have an old-fashioned flavor, even though they reflect today's attention to healthful baking.

Nonstick vegetable oil cooking spray, for the baking sheets

3¼ cups whole wheat pastry flour

1 cup rolled (old-fashioned) oats

1 teaspoon baking soda

½ teaspoon ground allspice

½ teaspoon fine sea salt

¾ cup liquid fruit juice concentrate or Fruit Juice Reduction (page 23)

¾ cup unsweetened applesauce

2 large egg whites, at room temperature

3 tablespoons canola oil

1 tablespoon vanilla extract

½ cup dried currants

1 Position racks in the center and top third of the oven and preheat the oven to 350° F. Lightly spray 2 baking sheets with vegetable oil spray.

2 In a medium bowl, whisk the flour, oats, baking soda, allspice, and salt to combine and make a well in the center.

3 In another medium bowl, whisk the fruit juice concentrate, applesauce, egg whites, oil, and vanilla until smooth. Pour into the well and stir with a wooden spoon just until a dough forms. Do not overmix. Stir in the currants. Drop by rounded tablespoons about 1½ inches apart onto the prepared baking sheets.

4 Bake until the edges of the cookies are lightly browned and the tops spring back when pressed lightly in the center with a finger, 12 to 15 minutes. Transfer to wire cake racks to cool completely.

Almond Jewel Cookies

Egg Free
Dairy Free
Whole Grain

Makes about 40 cookies

Filled with your favorite fruit-sweetened spread, these cookies are great at any time of year. They are absolutely unbeatable on a holiday cookie platter. Use your favorite flavor spread—try raspberry, blueberry, apricot, or cherry, or make a few cookies with each for variety.

Nonstick vegetable oil cooking spray, for the baking sheets

1¼ cups (5 ounces) sliced unblanched almonds, divided

2¾ cups whole wheat pastry flour, divided

1 cup maple sugar

1 teaspoon baking soda

½ teaspoon fine sea salt

½ cup plus 2 tablespoons liquid fruit juice concentrate or Fruit Juice Reduction (page 23)

½ cup Prune Butter (page 23)

3 tablespoons canola oil

1 tablespoon vanilla extract

¼ cup hot water

¼ cup soy milk

⅔ cup fruit-sweetened fruit spread

1 Position racks in the center and top third of the oven and preheat the oven to 350° F. Lightly spray 2 large baking sheets with vegetable oil spray.

2 In a blender, process ¼ cup of the almonds with *1 tablespoon* of the flour until ground to a fine meal. Transfer to a medium bowl. Add the *remaining* flour, the maple sugar, baking soda, and salt. Whisk well to combine, make a well in the center, and set aside. Process the *remaining 1 cup* almonds until coarsely chopped and transfer to a small bowl.

3 In a large bowl, using a handheld electric mixer set at high speed, beat the fruit juice concentrate, Prune Butter, oil, and vanilla until combined. Beat in the hot water until smooth. Pour in the well and stir with a wooden spoon just until the dough forms a soft dough. Do not overmix.

4 Using a level tablespoon of dough for each cookie, roll the dough into balls. Pour the soy milk into a small bowl. Roll each ball of dough in the soy milk, then roll in the chopped almonds, pressing the almonds into the dough. Place on the baking sheets about 2 inches apart. Holding the ball with your thumb and forefinger so the sides of the ball don't crack, press a ½-inch-deep impression in the center of each ball with the tip of your other thumb. If a ball cracks, reshape it and smooth the sides.

5 Bake until the cookies are set, about 10 minutes. Remove from the oven. In a small bowl, whisk the fruit spread until smooth. Spoon ½ teaspoon of the spread into the impression in each cookie. Return to the oven, switching the positions of the baking sheets from top to bottom. Bake until the sides of the cookies are firm when pressed with a finger, 2 to 3 minutes. Cool the cookies for 2 minutes on the baking sheets, then transfer to wire cake racks to cool completely.

Butter Spritz Cookies

Makes about 48 cookies

These butter cookies are fun to make, and they look beautiful, especially as part of an assortment of holiday cookies. Traditionally they would be decorated with candied fruits, but I prefer to use the dried cherries, blueberries, and cranberries available at specialty food shops and many supermarkets. Pecan halves would work well, too.

Parchment paper, for the baking sheets

About 48 (¼ cup) dried cherries, blueberries, or cranberries, for decoration

12 tablespoons (1½ sticks) unsalted butter, at room temperature

¾ cup maple sugar

½ cup liquid fruit juice concentrate or Fruit Juice Reduction (page 23)

2 large eggs, at room temperature

2¾ cups soft white unbleached pastry flour (page 19)

¼ teaspoon fine sea salt

1 Position racks in the top third and center of the oven and preheat the oven to 350° F. Line 2 baking sheets with parchment paper.

2 Place the dried fruit in a small bowl and add enough hot water to cover. Set aside while making the dough.

3 In a medium bowl, using a handheld electric mixer set at medium speed, beat the butter until creamy, about 1 minute. Add the maple sugar and fruit juice concentrate and beat until lighter in color, about 2 minutes. Beat in the eggs, one at a time, beating well after each addition.

4 Reduce the mixer speed to low. Add the flour and salt and mix just until a soft dough is formed. Transfer to a large pastry bag fitted with a large open star tip, such as Ateco Number 5. Pipe rosettes of the the dough about 1¼ inches wide and ½ inch high onto the baking sheets, spaced about 1 inch apart. Drain the fruit and pat dry with paper towels. Place a piece of fruit in the center of each cookie.

5 Bake until the edges of the cookies are beginning to brown, 12 to 15 minutes. Halfway through baking, switch the positions of the sheets from top to bottom. Cool completely on a wire cake rack.

Coconut Macaroons

Whole Grain

Makes 12 macaroons

Parchment paper, for the baking sheet

1¾ cups (6 ounces) unsweetened desiccated coconut

¾ cup plus 2 tablespoons maple sugar

3 large egg whites

2 tablespoons whole wheat pastry flour

⅛ teaspoon fine sea salt

Coconut macaroons are a cookie classic. I make mine with desiccated coconut flakes available at natural foods stores, not the sugary kind from the supermarket. These macaroons turn out golden and lightly crispy on the outside, moist and chewy within. If you like yours crispier throughout, bake for a few minutes longer.

1 Position a rack in the center of the oven and preheat the oven to 375° F. Line a large baking sheet with parchment paper.

2 In the top part of a double boiler or a medium heatproof bowl, combine the coconut, all the maple sugar, the egg whites, flour, and salt. Place the bowl over a medium saucepan of boiling water over low heat. Do not let the bottom of the bowl touch the water. Cook, stirring often, until the maple sugar is almost completely melted and the mixture is stiff enough to hold its shape when a small amount is formed into a mound, about 8 minutes.

3 Divide the dough into 12 portions and place on the baking sheet. Using a moistened finger, press each portion of dough into a kiss-shaped mound about 1¾ inches wide at the base.

4 Bake until the macaroons are golden brown, 12 to 15 minutes. Cool on a wire cake rack. Store the macaroons in an airtight container at room temperature.

Raspberry Linzer Cookies

Low Fat
Egg Free
Dairy Free
Wheat Free

Makes 10 large cookies

These cookies are really a mouthful: a full 3 inches across, filled with raspberry spread, and topped with a lattice of cookie dough. They will convert skeptics to healthful baking—they are fabulous even without wheat, eggs, dairy products, or excess fat! This recipe taught me a lesson about low-fat versus nonfat baking. The first time I made them, I tried for a fat-free version, and the results were flat-tasting and tough. The second version had a mere three tablespoons of canola oil, and the cookies sprang to life. I have learned that if the fat content is too low, baked goods suffer in flavor and texture.

Parchment paper, for the baking sheets

2¾ cups oat flour

1 teaspoon baking soda

¼ teaspoon fine sea salt

¾ cup maple sugar

½ cup Prune Butter (page 23)

½ cup liquid fruit juice concentrate or Fruit Juice Reduction (page 23)

¼ cup hot water

Grated zest of 1 lemon

3 tablespoons fresh lemon juice

3 tablespoons canola oil

½ cup fruit-sweetened raspberry spread

1 Position a rack in the center of the oven and preheat the oven to 350° F. Line 2 baking sheets with parchment paper.

2 Sift together the flour, baking soda, and salt into a medium bowl. Whisk in the maple sugar and make a well in the center.

3 In another medium bowl, whisk the Prune Butter, fruit juice concentrate, hot water, lemon zest, lemon juice, and canola oil until combined. Pour into the well and stir with a wooden spoon just until mixed. Do not overmix.

4 Using 2 tablespoons of dough for each cookie, roll into 10 balls and place about 3 inches apart on the baking sheets. Transfer the remaining dough to a pastry bag fitted with a plain tip about ⅜ inch wide, such as Ateco Number 3, and set aside. Using the back of a tablespoon dipped in water, make an indentation about 1¼ inches wide in the center of each cookie. Fill each with about 2 teaspoons of the spread. Pipe a lattice pattern across the tops of the cookies with the dough in the pastry bag.

5 Bake until the edges of the cookies are lightly browned, 15 to 18 minutes. Cool completely on wire cake racks.

Almond Shortbread

Egg Free

Makes 8 large cookies

Butter, for the pan

1½ cups (6 ounces) sliced almonds

1 cup whole wheat pastry flour, divided

1 cup soft white unbleached pastry flour (page 20)

14 tablespoons (1¾ sticks) unsalted butter, softened

½ cup maple sugar

Simple to make, this shortbread is melt-in-your-mouth buttery yet crumbly, pure heaven with a hot cup of tea. It is Scotland's contribution to the pastry hall of fame. Ground almonds make this version special. Sometimes I chocolate-dip these, as described on page 64.

1 Position a rack in the center of the oven and preheat the oven to 375° F. Lightly butter a 9-inch springform pan.

2 In a food processor fitted with the metal blade or in a blender in 2 batches, pulse the almonds with *2 tablespoons* of the whole wheat pastry flour until finely ground into a meal. Transfer to a bowl and add the *remaining* whole wheat pastry flour and unbleached pastry flour; whisk to combine.

3 In a medium bowl, using a handheld electric mixer set at medium speed, beat the butter until smooth, about 1 minute. Add the maple sugar and beat until the mixture is lighter in color, about 2 minutes. Using a wooden spoon, stir in the flour mixture to form a stiff dough. Press the dough firmly and evenly into the prepared pan. Using a fork, prick the dough to mark into 8 equal wedges.

4 Bake until the edges are lightly browned and beginning to shrink from the sides of the pan, 20 to 25 minutes. Cool on a wire cake rack for 5 minutes. Remove the sides of the pan. Using a thin-bladed sharp knife, cut through the markings to divide the shortbread into wedges. Cool completely on the wire rack.

Ginger Happy Face Cookies

Low Fat
Egg Free
Whole Grain

Makes about 22 large cookies

This is a great kitchen project for kids, as they can whimsically decorate the cookies with currants and raisins. The spicy flavor is akin to gingerbread, but the dough doesn't have to be chilled and rolled out, making these easy to bake up on a rainy afternoon. Because of their reduced-fat nature, they can dry out if overbaked, so bake only until the edges are lightly browned.

Nonstick vegetable oil cooking spray, for the baking sheets

½ cup liquid fruit juice concentrate or Fruit Juice Reduction (page 23)

½ cup Prune Butter (page 23)

4 tablespoons (½ stick) unsalted butter, at room temperature

1 tablespoon vanilla extract

1 cup maple sugar

3 cups whole wheat pastry flour

2 teaspoons ground ginger

1 teaspoon ground cinnamon

¼ teaspoon ground cloves

1 teaspoon baking soda

½ teaspoon fine sea salt

Dried currants and raisins, for decoration

1 Position racks in the top third and center of the oven and preheat the oven to 350° F. Lightly spray 2 baking sheets with vegetable oil spray.

2 In a large bowl, using a handheld electric mixer set at medium speed, beat the fruit juice concentrate, Prune Butter, butter, and vanilla until combined. Beat in the maple sugar.

3 In a large bowl, whisk the flour, ginger, cinnamon, cloves, baking soda, and salt to combine. Add to the creamed mixture and stir with a wooden spoon to form a stiff dough.

4 Using moistened hands, form the dough into 1½-inch balls (about 2 level tablespoons of dough each). Place the balls about 3 inches apart on the baking sheets. Using the bottom of a flat, wide glass dipped in cold water, press the balls to form cookies about 3 inches wide and ¼ inch thick. Press the currants and raisins into the cookies to form smiling faces with eyes, nose, and a mouth.

5 Bake just until the cookies spring back when pressed in the center, about 15 minutes. Halfway through baking, switch the position of the baking sheets from top to bottom. Cool on wire cake racks.

A Celebration of Cakes

Serving a beautifully decorated and frosted layer cake is a special event that occurs at celebrations like birthdays or holiday meals. Unfortunately, your birthday isn't every day. It just isn't necessary to have a slice of iced cake every day, but for a festive affair, you should be able to serve a fancy cake unapologetically. I don't believe in trying to remake a pleasure-filled cake into something it shouldn't be, namely low fat. So, once in a while, have a slice of Banana Layer Cake with Cream Cheese Frosting, Hollywood Cheesecake, or Mocha Almond Cake.

For less special occasions, a slice of a simple homemade cake is still one of life's great pleasures, and that is the time to go with a reduced fat version. Try the Black Forest Bundt Cake, a deep chocolate cake studded with cherries or raspberries, for an example of just how good my reduced-fat cakes can be. Even an all-American classic upside-down cake can get a modern twist like my Blackberry Upside-Down Cake. And you don't have to be on a restricted diet to enjoy the Chunky Carrot Cake.

Organization is the key to successful baking, particularly when making cakes. Here are some of my tips: ❦ Always turn on the oven to preheat while gathering the ingredients so it will preheat to the proper temperature at the same time that the batter is ready. Buy an oven thermometer to hang on the oven rack to double check that the temperature is correct. The mercury-registered glass thermometers are more accurate than the spring-operated kind.

Chocolate Raspberry Fortress Cake

Black Forest Bundt Cake

Low Fat
Whole Grain

When creating low-fat desserts, it's important to have contrasting layers of flavor to add interest. This rich chocolate cake, for example, gets a cherry and walnut filling that lifts it out of the ordinary.

Makes 10 to 12 servings

Butter and all-purpose flour, for the pan

2 cups whole wheat pastry flour

1 cup natural cocoa powder (not Dutch process)

1 teaspoon baking powder

¼ teaspoon fine sea salt

1½ cups maple sugar

2 large eggs

1 large egg white

1 cup Prune Butter (page 23)

1 cup skim milk

2 teaspoons vanilla extract

2 tablespoons instant espresso powder

2 teaspoons baking soda

1 cup boiling water

1 cup coarsely chopped pitted fresh or unthawed frozen sweet cherries or raspberries

½ cup chopped walnuts

1 Position a rack in the center of the oven and preheat the oven to 350° F. Butter well and flour a 10-inch bundt pan, tapping out excess flour.

2 Sift the flour, cocoa, baking powder, and salt into a medium bowl. Whisk in the maple sugar. Make a well in the center.

3 In another medium bowl, whisk the eggs and egg white. Add the Prune Butter, milk, and vanilla and whisk until well combined. Pour into the well and whisk just to combine.

4 Dissolve the espresso and baking soda in the boiling water. Pour into the batter and whisk until smooth. Pour half of the batter into the pan. Sprinkle with the cherries and walnuts. Gently spoon in the remaining batter. (This will keep the cherries and walnuts suspended in the center of the cake. If the batter is poured in, they will rise to the top.) Using a metal spatula, smooth the top.

5 Bake until a long wooden skewer inserted in the center of the cake comes out clean, 50 to 60 minutes. Cool on a wire cake rack for 15 minutes. Invert the cake onto the cake rack and unmold. Cool completely. *(Covered tightly with plastic wrap and stored at room temperature, the cake will keep for up to 2 days.)*

Banana Layer Cake
with Cream Cheese Frosting

Whole Grain

Makes 10 to 12 servings

I've always loved spreading cream cheese onto sliced banana bread, and I couldn't resist the temptation to upgrade the combination into a layer cake. I added sliced bananas between the layers for a stronger banana flavor and used blueberry spread for contrast. The fruity filling cuts down on the amount of frosting needed, so the cake doesn't become too heavy or cloying.

BANANA CAKE

Butter and all-purpose flour, for pan

2 cups whole wheat pastry flour

1 teaspoon baking soda

1 teaspoon ground cinnamon

¼ teaspoon ground ginger

¼ teaspoon fine sea salt

1¼ cups liquid fruit juice concentrate or Fruit Juice Reduction (page 23)

1 cup mashed very ripe bananas (3 medium bananas)

½ cup canola oil

2 large eggs, at room temperature

1 teaspoon vanilla extract

CREAM CHEESE FROSTING

1 pound cream cheese, at room temperature

½ cup liquid fruit juice concentrate or Fruit Juice Reduction (page 23)

1 tablespoon vanilla extract

1 cup fruit-sweetened blueberry spread

2 small ripe bananas, thinly sliced

8 pecan halves, for decoration

1 To make the cake: Position a rack in the center of the oven and preheat the oven to 350° F. Lightly butter and flour a 9-inch springform pan, tapping out excess flour.

2 Sift together the flour, baking soda, cinnamon, ginger, and salt into a medium bowl. Make a well in the center.

3 In another medium bowl, using a handheld electric mixer at medium speed, beat the fruit juice concentrate, bananas, oil, eggs, and vanilla until well combined. Pour into the dry ingredients. With the mixer set at medium speed, beat until smooth, scraping down the sides of the bowl with a rubber spatula as necessary. Pour the batter into the pan and smooth the top.

4 Bake until a toothpick inserted in the center of the cake comes out clean, about 35 minutes. Let the cake cool on a wire cake rack for 5 minutes. Remove the sides of the pan, invert onto the rack, and remove the pan bottom. Set the cake right side up and cool completely.

5 To make the frosting: In a medium bowl, using a handheld electric mixer set at medium speed, beat the cream cheese until absolutely smooth and lump-free. Reduce the speed to low and gradually beat in the fruit juice concentrate, then the vanilla. Reserve ⅔ cup of the frosting. Transfer the *remaining* frosting to a pastry bag fitted with a large star tip, such as Ateco Number 5.

6 To assemble: Using a long serrated knife, cut the cake horizontally into 3 layers. Place a dab of the frosting in the center of a serving plate. Place the bottom cake layer on the plate. Use about one-fourth of the frosting in the pastry bag to pipe a border around the perimeter of the cake layer. Spread the top of the cake inside the border with half of the blueberry spread, then top with half of the banana slices. Top with the second cake layer and press lightly. Pipe a border of icing around the perimeter of that layer, spread with the remaining blueberry spread, and top with the remaining bananas. Top with the final layer, right side up. Spread the top of the cake smoothly with the reserved frosting. Use the remaining frosting in the pastry bag to pipe 8 stars or rosettes on top of the cake as decorations. Place a pecan half on top of each frosting star. Cover the cake with plastic wrap and refrigerate until ready to serve. *(The finished cake can be prepared up to 1 day ahead, covered loosely in plastic wrap or placed in a large lidded cake holder, and refrigerated. Remove the cake from the refrigerator at least 1 hour before serving.)*

Blackberry Upside-Down Cake

Whole Grain

Makes 10 servings

An American classic, upside-down cake, gets a makeover with blackberries replacing the familiar canned pineapple rings. This is another dessert that is at its best when served warm from the oven.

Nonstick vegetable oil cooking spray, for the pan

FRUIT

⅓ cup liquid fruit juice concentrate or Fruit Juice Reduction (page 23)

2 tablespoons canola oil

3 cups (1½ pints) fresh or unthawed frozen blackberries

CAKE

3 large egg whites, at room temperature

¾ cup liquid fruit juice concentrate or Fruit Juice Reduction (page 23)

⅔ cup skim milk

⅓ cup plus 1 tablespoon canola oil

2 teaspoons vanilla extract

2 cups whole wheat pastry flour

2 teaspoons baking powder

¼ teaspoon fine sea salt

1 Position a rack in the center of the oven and preheat the oven to 350° F. Spray a 10-inch ovenproof skillet or springform pan with vegetable oil spray.

2 **To make the fruit layer:** In a small non-reactive saucepan over medium heat, bring the fruit juice concentrate and oil to a simmer. Reduce the heat to low and simmer for 2 minutes. Pour into the prepared pan. Immediately arrange the blackberries in the pan in a single layer. Work quickly, as the syrup will harden rapidly. Place in the freezer while preparing the batter. (This will keep the fruit from floating to the top of the batter during baking.)

3 **To make the cake:** In a grease-free medium bowl, using a handheld electric mixer at high speed, beat the egg whites until soft peaks form. Gradually beat in the fruit juice concentrate, beating until stiff peaks form. Reduce the speed to low and add the milk, oil, and vanilla, mixing until well combined.

4 In another medium bowl, whisk the flour, baking powder, and salt until combined. Add to the liquid ingredients and whisk until smooth. Remove the pan from the freezer and pour the batter over the fruit.

5 Bake until a toothpick inserted in the center comes out clean, 35 to 40 minutes. Cool on a cake rack for 10 minutes. Run a knife around the inside of the skillet or springform to loosen the cake. Invert onto a serving plate. Let stand for 5 minutes so the cake can absorb the juices. Remove the skillet or release the sides of the springform and carefully lift off the bottom. Serve the cake warm or at room temperature.

Chocolate Raspberry Fortress Cake

Makes 12 servings

Chocolate and raspberries are a classic combination that is hard to beat, and they are especially enjoyable in this towering creation. It is the most popular cake at Mäni's Bakery. At the bakery, we surround the sides of the cake with a band of chocolate which is a very complicated procedure; the chocolate chip decoration is much easier. A few years ago, our talented bakers made one large enough to feed a hundred people with "Roseanne" inscribed on top to celebrate the show's one hundredth episode at a cast and crew party.

CHOCOLATE CAKE

Butter and all-purpose flour, for the pan

2¼ cups unbleached all-purpose flour

¾ cup natural cocoa powder (not Dutch process)

½ teaspoon fine sea salt

8 tablespoons (1 stick) unsalted butter, at room temperature

1¼ cups liquid fruit juice concentrate or Fruit Juice Reduction (page 23)

2 teaspoons vanilla extract

1 tablespoon baking soda

1 cup boiling water

3 large eggs, beaten together, at room temperature

1 Position a rack in the center of the oven and preheat the oven to 350° F. Butter and flour the sides of a 10-inch springform pan, tapping out excess flour. Line the bottom of the pan with a round of wax paper.

2 **To make the chocolate cake:** Sift the flour, cocoa, and salt together into a medium bowl. In a large bowl, using a handheld electric mixer set at high speed, beat the butter, fruit juice concentrate, and vanilla until well combined, about 1 minute. Reduce the speed to low. Beat in the flour mixture. The batter will be thick.

3 In a measuring cup, dissolve the baking soda in the boiling water. Alternating in thirds, starting with the eggs and ending with the water, beat the eggs and water into the batter, beating well after each addition and scraping down the sides of the bowl as needed with a rubber spatula. Transfer to the pan and smooth the top.

4 Bake until a toothpick inserted in the center of the cake comes out clean and the top springs back when pressed with a finger, about 40 minutes. Cool in the pan for 5 minutes. Remove the sides of the pan, then invert onto a wire cake rack. Remove the pan bottom and carefully peel off the wax paper. Invert right side up and cool completely on the cake rack.

5 **To make the mousse frosting:** In a small nonreactive saucepan over low heat, heat the fruit juice concentrate and honey just until warm. Do not boil. Remove from the heat. Add the chocolate chips and let stand until the chips are softened, about 5 minutes. Add the vanilla and whisk until smooth. Cool, stirring occasionally, until tepid, about 10 minutes.

6 Place the cream in a chilled large bowl and sift in the cocoa. Beat the cream until soft peaks form. Add the cooled chocolate mixture and beat until stiff. Use a rubber spatula to be sure that no chocolate is at the bottom of the bowl and fold a few times to combine, if necessary. (Do not overbeat the cream, or you may get chocolate butter!) Transfer a heaping cup of the frosting to a pastry bag fitted with a large star tip, such as Ateco Number 5. Refrigerate the remaining frosting and the pastry bag until ready to use.

MOUSSE FROSTING

3 tablespoons liquid fruit juice concentrate or Fruit Juice Reduction (page 23)

2 tablespoons honey

¼ cup (1½ ounces) malt-sweetened semisweet chocolate chips

1 tablespoon vanilla extract

2⅓ cups heavy cream, well chilled

¼ cup natural cocoa powder (not Dutch process)

2 cups (two 6-ounce baskets) raspberries, **divided**

1 cup (6 ounces) malt-sweetened semisweet chocolate chips, for decoration

7 **To assemble:** Using a long serrated knife, level the top of the cake by slicing off the domed top and set aside for another use. (Cut it into wedges for a snack, for example.) Slice the remaining cake in half horizontally. Place the bottom layer on a serving platter and spread with one-third of the remaining frosting. Sprinkle with *three-fourths* of the raspberries and press the berries into the frosting. Top with the second layer. Spread the top and sides with the remaining frosting. Using the pastry bag, decorate the top of the cake with swirls and rosettes.

8 In a food processor fitted with the metal blade, pulse the chocolate chips until finely chopped. Press the chopped chips around the sides of the cake. Garnish the top of the cake with the *remaining* raspberries. *(The cake can be prepared up to 8 hours ahead, covered with plastic wrap or placed in a large lidded cake holder, and refrigerated. To keep the plastic wrap from touching and marring the frosting, stick a few toothpicks in the cake and tent the wrap around the cake.)* Serve chilled.

Modern Mini Fruitcakes

Low Fat
Whole Grain

Makes five
5½ x 3¼-inch loaves

I know why fruitcakes get a bad rap—who wants to eat all of those sugary, Day-Glo–colored dried fruits? But I can't resist a spicy whole wheat cake chock-full of fresh pineapple, cranberries, and currants. Because this cake is such a natural for holiday gift-giving, I bake it in mini loaves to offer as presents.

Butter and all-purpose flour, for the pans

1½ cups fresh pineapple chunks, about 1 x 1 x ½ inch, or 1 can (8 ounces) pineapple chunks in juice, drained

1 cup fresh or unthawed frozen cranberries

1 cup dried currants

½ cup chopped pecans

1⅔ cups liquid fruit juice concentrate or Fruit Juice Reduction (page 23)

1 cup buttermilk

3 large eggs

3 cups whole wheat pastry flour

1½ teaspoons baking soda

½ teaspoon fine sea salt

½ teaspoon ground cinnamon

¼ teaspoon ground ginger

¼ teaspoon ground allspice

1 Position a rack in the center of the oven and preheat the oven to 350° F. Lightly butter and flour five 5½ x 3¼ x 2-inch mini loaf pans, tapping out the excess flour.

2 In a medium bowl, combine the pineapple, cranberries, currants, and pecans. Measure out ¾ cup of the mixture and set aside.

3 In another medium bowl, whisk the fruit juice concentrate, buttermilk, and eggs until well combined. Sift the flour, baking soda, salt, cinnamon, ginger, and allspice into another medium bowl. Add to the wet ingredients and whisk until smooth. Stir in the remaining fruit-pecan mixture. Divide the batter evenly among the pans, smoothing the tops. Sprinkle the reserved fruit-pecan mixture over the tops of the mini loaves. Place the pans on a large baking sheet.

4 Bake until the tops of the loaves spring back when pressed lightly with a finger, 45 to 55 minutes. Cool for 10 minutes on a wire cake rack. Run a knife around the insides of the pans to loosen the cakes, then unmold onto the cake rack. Cool completely. *(Wrapped tightly in plastic wrap, the loaves will keep at room temperature for up to 3 days.)*

Hollywood Cheesecake

Makes 12 servings

This bears a distinct resemblance to the classic New York cheesecake, but of course mine is made without sugar. It gets its refreshing taste from a mere hint of citrus peel—not enough to call it a lemon-orange cheesecake but enough to tease your tastebuds.

CRUST

Butter, for the pan

1 ½ cups graham cracker crumbs, preferably made from fruit juice–sweetened crackers

5 tablespoons unsalted butter, melted

FILLING

2 pounds cream cheese, at room temperature

1 ½ cups liquid fruit juice concentrate or Fruit Juice Reduction (page 23)

4 large eggs, at room temperature

Grated zest of 1 lemon

Grated zest of ½ orange

3 tablespoons sour cream

1 teaspoon vanilla extract

1 **To make the crust:** Position a rack in the center of the oven and preheat the oven to 350° F. Lightly butter a 9-inch springform pan.

2 In a medium bowl, mix the crumbs and butter until well combined. Press the crumb mixture firmly and evenly into the pan. Bake until the edges of the crust are lightly browned, 10 to 12 minutes. Remove the pan from the oven.

3 **To make the filling:** In a medium bowl, using a handheld electric mixer set at medium speed, beat the cream cheese well until absolutely smooth and lump-free. With the mixer on low speed, gradually beat in the fruit juice concentrate. Beat in the eggs, one at a time. Add the grated zests, sour cream, and vanilla and beat until mixed. Pour into the prepared crust and smooth the top.

4 Bake for 10 minutes. Reduce the oven temperature to 275° F. and continue baking until the edges of the filling are puffed and lightly browned, about 1 hour. The center of the cheesecake may seem not completely set, but it will firm upon cooling and chilling. Turn off the oven. Run a sharp knife around the inside of the pan to release the cheesecake from the sides. Let the cheesecake cool completely in the turned-off oven. If you need to use the oven, cool the cheesecake on a wire cake rack.

5 Cover the cheesecake with plastic wrap and refrigerate for at least 8 hours or overnight. Remove the sides of the pan. Serve the cheesecake chilled, dipping the knife into a glass of hot water before slicing each piece. *(The cheesecake can be prepared up to 3 days ahead, wrapped tightly in plastic wrap, and refrigerated.)*

Fruit Glaze Topping: The top of the cheesecake can be glazed with any fruit-sweetened spread that you wish—strawberry, blueberry, and apricot are especially good. In a small saucepan over low heat, heat ½ cup fruit spread, stirring just until melted. Spread the top of the chilled cheesecake with the spread and refrigerate until set, about 10 minutes.

Chocolate-Walnut Topping: Toast 1 cup (4 ounces) walnuts on a baking sheet in a preheated 350° F. oven, stirring occasionally, until lightly toasted, about 10 minutes. Cool the walnuts completely, then coarsely chop them. In the top part of a double boiler over hot, not simmering water, melt 6 ounces (1 cup) malt-sweetened semisweet chocolate chips. Drizzle half of the chocolate around the perimeter of the cheesecake. Sprinkle with the walnuts. Drizzle the walnuts with the remaining chocolate. Refrigerate until the topping is set, about 10 minutes.

Chunky Carrot Cake

Egg Free
Dairy Free

Makes 8 to 10 servings

Egg-free cakes are a hard shell to crack (sorry!), but for the growing number of people who are choosing to omit eggs from their diets, this carrot cake is a good choice. The carrots add moisture that would otherwise be supplied by the eggs. At Mäni's Bakery we omit the nuts, but I add them here for crunch. If you wish, frost the cake with Cream Cheese Frosting (page 83), but the plain cake is also fine in its spicy simplicity.

Butter and all-purpose flour, for pan

1½ cups whole wheat pastry flour

1 cup unbleached all-purpose flour

1 teaspoon baking soda

1 teaspoon ground cinnamon

½ teaspoon ground ginger

½ teaspoon grated nutmeg

½ teaspoon baking powder

¼ teaspoon fine sea salt

1 cup liquid fruit juice concentrate or Fruit Juice Reduction (page 23)

¾ cup canola oil

¼ cup fresh lemon juice

2 cups shredded carrots (5 medium carrots)

1 cup coarsely chopped walnuts or pecans

½ cup raisins

1 Position a rack in the center of the oven and preheat the oven to 350° F. Lightly butter and flour a 9-inch tube pan, tapping out excess flour. Line the bottom of the pan with a ring of wax paper.

2 Sift together the whole wheat pastry flour, unbleached flour, baking soda, cinnamon, ginger, nutmeg, baking powder, and salt into a large bowl and make a well in the center.

3 In another bowl, whisk the fruit juice concentrate, oil, and lemon juice. Pour the liquids into the well and stir until smooth. Stir in the carrots, walnuts, and raisins. Pour into the pan and smooth the top.

4 Bake until a toothpick inserted in the center of the cake comes out clean and the sides begin to pull away from the sides of the pan, 30 to 35 minutes. Cool the cake on a wire cake rack for 5 minutes. Invert and unmold the cake onto the rack, carefully remove the wax paper, and cool completely.

Mocha Almond Cake

Makes 12 servings

Arnold Elser was head baker at Mäni's for many years. His recipe for this coffee-scented layer cake, slathered in buttercream and surrounded with a crisp almond nougat, reminds me of something you'd get in a European café, which is no surprise as Arnold is Swiss born and trained.

CAKE

Butter and all-purpose flour, for the pans

¾ cup (3 ounces) blanched or unblanched sliced almonds

1¾ cups unbleached all-purpose flour, divided

8 tablespoons (1 stick) unsalted butter, at room temperature

1 cup liquid fruit juice concentrate or Fruit Juice Reduction (page 23)

3 large eggs, at room temperature

1 tablespoon vanilla extract

1 tablespoon baking soda

⅔ cup boiling water

ALMOND NOUGAT

Nonstick vegetable oil cooking spray, for the baking sheet

2 tablespoons unsalted butter

2 tablespoons liquid fruit juice concentrate or Fruit Juice Reduction (page 23)

1½ cups (6 ounces) blanched or unblanched sliced almonds

1 **To make the cake:** Position a rack in the center of the oven and preheat the oven to 350° F. Butter and flour two 8-inch round cake pans, tapping out excess flour. Line the bottoms of the pans with rounds of wax paper.

2 In a food processor fitted with the metal blade, combine the almonds and *2 tablespoons* of the flour. Pulse the machine until the almonds are finely ground into a meal. Transfer to a medium bowl. Sift the *remaining* flour into the bowl and whisk the flour and almond meal to combine.

3 In a medium bowl, using a handheld electric mixer set at high speed, beat the butter until smooth and creamy, about 1 minute. Gradually beat in the fruit juice concentrate. Beat in the eggs, one at a time, beating well after each addition. Beat in the vanilla.

4 Dissolve the baking soda in the boiling water. On low speed, alternating in thirds, starting with the liquid and ending with the flour, add the flour mixture and the liquid, beating just until the batter is smooth. Pour into the pans and smooth the tops.

5 Bake until a toothpick inserted in the center of the cakes comes out clean, 20 to 25 minutes. Cool on a wire cake rack for 5 minutes. Invert the cakes onto the racks and unmold. Carefully peel off the wax paper. Cool completely. *(The cakes can be prepared up to 1 day ahead, covered tightly with plastic wrap, and stored at room temperature.)*

6 **To make the almond nougat:** Spray a baking sheet with vegetable oil spray. In a heavy-bottomed medium nonreactive saucepan, melt the butter over medium heat. Stir in the fruit juice concentrate and bring to a simmer. Stir in the almonds. Cook, stirring often, until the liquid is thickened and beginning to caramelize, about 2 minutes. Spread in a thin layer on the baking sheet. Cool completely. *(The nougat can be prepared up to 4 hours ahead and stored, uncovered, at room temperature. Do not cover, or the almonds will get sticky.)*

Recipe continues on page 94.

ESPRESSO BUTTERCREAM

¾ cup liquid fruit juice concentrate or Fruit Juice Reduction (page 23)

3 large eggs, at room temperature

1 pound (4 sticks) unsalted butter, at room temperature

2 teaspoons instant espresso powder dissolved in 2 tablespoons boiling water, cooled

½ cup fruit-sweetened apricot spread (optional)

12 whole roasted coffee beans, for decoration (optional)

7 **To make the buttercream:** In a small nonreactive saucepan over medium heat, bring the fruit juice concentrate to a boil. In the bowl of a heavy-duty stand mixer fitted with the whisk blade, beat the eggs at medium-low speed until foamy. With the machine running, gradually pour the hot concentrate down the inside of the bowl. (Do not pour the hot concentrate directly into the blades, or it will splash and burn you.) Continue beating until the bottom of the bowl feels cool, about 7 minutes. Change to the paddle attachment. Beat in the butter, 1 tablespoon at a time. Beat in the espresso liquid. (The buttercream can also be prepared with a handheld electric mixer in a medium bowl, although using a handheld mixer will probably add about 5 minutes to the beating and cooling time. Place the bowl on a wire cake rack while beating so air can circulate under it and the mixture can cool more quickly.) Transfer about 2/3 cup of the buttercream to a pastry bag fitted with a large star tip, such as Ateco Number 5.

8 **To assemble:** Place 1 cake layer upside down on a serving platter. First spread with the apricot spread, if desired. Spread with about ½ cup of the buttercream. Top with the second cake layer, right side up. Frost the top, then the sides, of the cake with the remaining buttercream. Press the almond nougat around the sides of the cake. Use the pastry bag to pipe 12 large rosettes around the top of the cake. If desired, place a coffee bean on each rosette. Place the cake in the refrigerator to firm the buttercream. *(The finished cake can be prepared up to 1 day ahead, covered loosely in plastic wrap or placed in a large lidded cake holder, and refrigerated. Remove the cake from the refrigerator at least 1 hour before serving.)* Serve at room temperature.

Strawberry Shortcakes

with Mäni's Special Strawberry Sauce

Egg Free

Makes 6 servings

Strawberry shortcake is a summertime joy. My strawberry sauce is radical in its use of frozen berries. The strawberry variety used for frozen berries was developed to retain its taste during the freezing process, so your sauce will not be inferior in the least. However, the shortcake should be topped with fresh berries, so look for the reddest, plumpest, most fragrant ones you can find. The secret to tender shortcake is to handle the dough lightly—no kneading allowed!

STRAWBERRY SAUCE

1 bag (20 ounces) unsweetened frozen strawberries, thawed

½ cup liquid fruit juice concentrate or Fruit Juice Reduction (page 23)

1 tablespoon fresh lemon juice

SHORTCAKES

1¾ cups unbleached all-purpose flour

1 tablespoon baking powder

½ teaspoon fine sea salt

5 tablespoons unsalted butter, chilled, cut into ½-inch cubes

¾ cup milk plus extra for brushing

2 tablespoons liquid fruit juice concentrate or Fruit Juice Reduction (page 23)

1 cup heavy (whipping) cream, chilled

⅓ cup liquid fruit juice concentrate, or Fruit Juice Reduction (page 23)

1 teaspoon vanilla extract

2 pints fresh strawberries, sliced

1 **To make the sauce:** Place the thawed strawberries in a sieve placed over a tall bowl. Place in the refrigerator and let drain for at least 2 hours, preferably overnight. Pour the drained liquid into a small nonreactive saucepan. Boil over high heat until reduced to ¼ cup, about 10 minutes.

2 In a blender, process the drained strawberries, fruit juice concentrate, reduced strawberry liquid, and lemon juice until pureed. Pour into a medium bowl, cover with plastic wrap, and refrigerate until ready to use.

3 **To make the shortcakes:** Position a rack in the center of the oven and preheat the oven to 400° F. Set aside an ungreased baking sheet.

4 In a medium bowl, whisk the flour, baking powder, and salt to combine. Add the butter. Using a wire pastry blender or 2 forks, cut in the butter until the mixture resembles coarse meal. Make a well in the center and add the milk and fruit juice concentrate. Stir just to make a soft dough.

5 On a lightly floured work surface, pat or roll out the dough ½ inch thick. Using a 3¼-inch round biscuit cutter or an inverted drinking glass, cut out the shortcakes. Gather up the scraps, knead very briefly to combine, and repeat the rolling and cutting out until all of the dough has been used. Transfer the shortcakes to the baking sheet and brush the tops lightly with milk.

6 Bake until the shortcakes are risen and the tops are golden brown, about 15 minutes. Cool slightly. Cut the shortcakes in half horizontally.

7 In a chilled medium bowl, beat the cream, ⅓ cup fruit juice concentrate and vanilla just until stiff peaks form. In another medium bowl, combine the strawberries with ½ cup of the strawberry sauce.

8 Place each shortcake bottom on a dessert plate. Spoon the strawberries evenly over, then top with the whipped cream. Replace the tops and pour the remaining strawberry sauce around the shortcakes. Serve immediately.

Upper Crust Pies and Tarts
(plus Turnovers and a Cobbler, too)

These pies and tarts are brimming with the natural goodness of fresh fruits. And what better way to sweeten a fruit-based dessert than with a fruit-based sweetener? Apples, berries, even an accent of fresh citrus zest assert their flavors more clearly than would be possible with the overpowering sweetness of sugar.

If you choose to eliminate the fat, two of my pie fillings—Pear Frangipane Custard and Apple-Yogurt Custard—can be baked in lightly oiled pie plates without a crust. Pies and tarts do lend themselves to working within the limitations of other dietary restrictions—the Apple Tart with Yogurt Custard in a Walnut-Oat Crust, for example, is wheat free.

When a whole wheat pie dough, even one prepared with low-gluten whole wheat pastry flour, is baked, the crust is crisp rather than flaky. As many people appreciate the flavor, texture, and nutritive value of a whole wheat crust, some of these desserts use it. For those bakers who prefer a more traditional flaky texture, I offer my New-Fashioned Pie Dough, which combines whole wheat and soft white pastry flours for a tender crust with better nutritive value than an all-white flour version. In any of the whole wheat pastry dough recipes, you may substitute soft white pastry flour for half of the whole wheat pastry flour for a less crisp crust.

Fresh Strawberry Tartlets

New-Fashioned Pie Dough

Egg Free

**Makes enough dough
for a single-crust
9- to 10-inch pie**

¾ cup unbleached soft white
pastry flour

¾ cup whole wheat pastry flour

¼ teaspoon fine sea salt

Scant ¼ teaspoon baking powder

8 tablespoons (1 stick) unsalted
butter or margarine, chilled, cut
into bits

6 tablespoons ice water

¼ teaspoon cider vinegar

Whole wheat pie crusts have a hearty taste but can be a bit too heavy for some palates. This recipe combines unbleached soft white flour and whole wheat pastry flour to give flakier results than a one hundred percent whole wheat crust and more nutrition than a completely white flour crust. The secret ingredients are just enough baking powder to lightly leaven the dough and a dash of vinegar, whose acid helps tenderize the gluten in the flour. If you are avoiding dairy products, use margarine in place of the butter.

1 In a medium bowl, whisk the unbleached and whole wheat pastry flours, salt, and baking powder to mix.

2 Add the butter. Using a pastry blender or 2 forks, cut the butter into the flour until the mixture resembles coarse crumbs.

3 In a small bowl, combine the ice water and vinegar. Stirring with a fork, gradually add the ice water mixture, until the dough is moist enough to hold together when pinched between your thumb and forefinger. You may need more or less ice water to moisten the dough, and the dough need not form into a ball.

4 Gather up the dough, flatten into a flat disk and wrap in wax paper. Refrigerate until just chilled, 20 to 30 minutes. *(The dough may be prepared up to 2 days ahead. Remove the dough from the refrigerator and let stand at room temperature until soft enough to roll without cracking, about 10 minutes.)*

Double Crust New-Fashioned Pie Dough:
Follow the directions above, using 1 cup *each* soft white pastry and whole wheat pastry flour, ¼ teaspoon salt, ¼ teaspoon baking powder, 10 tablespoons (1¼ sticks) unsalted butter, ½ cup ice water and ½ teaspoon vinegar. Gather up one-third of the dough into a thick disk. Flatten the remaining two-thirds into another disk. Wrap each disk in wax paper and chill.

Apple Turnovers

Egg Free

Makes 4 turnovers

Few desserts are as satisfying as baked apple turnovers fresh from the oven. Try these topped with a scoop of Vanilla Bean Ice Milk (page 116).

⅓ cup liquid fruit juice concentrate or Fruit Juice Reduction (page 23)

3 tablespoons unbleached all-purpose flour

1 teaspoon ground cinnamon

3 medium-size tart apples, such as Granny Smith, peeled, cored, and cut into ½-inch square pieces (about 2½ cups)

2 teaspoons fresh lemon juice

New-Fashioned Pie Dough (page 98)

Milk, for brushing

1 In a small bowl, combine the fruit juice concentrate, flour, and cinnamon. Cover and refrigerate until slightly thickened, at least 1 hour. In a medium bowl, toss the apples with the lemon juice, cover, and refrigerate until ready to use.

2 Position a rack in the top third of the oven and preheat the oven to 375° F.

3 On a lightly floured work surface, roll out the dough into a 15-inch square about ⅛ inch thick. Using a ruler and a sharp knife, cut the dough into four 7-inch squares.

4 Place 1 pastry square on a large baking sheet. Place one-fourth of the apple mixture in the center of the square. Spoon about 1½ tablespoons of the chilled fruit juice concentrate mixture over the apples. Fold the pastry over to form a triangle, pressing the edges of the dough with a fork to seal. Prick the top of the turnover with the fork and brush lightly with a little milk. Repeat the procedure with the remaining pastry squares, apples, and fruit juice concentrate mixture.

5 Bake until the pastry is golden brown, 25 to 30 minutes. Serve the turnovers hot, warm, or at room temperature.

Peach Foldover Pie

Egg Free

Makes 8 servings

This method gives you a double-crust pie without having to roll out two crusts, and it has a lovely rustic look, too. Be careful to choose ripe fragrant fresh peaches to make a pie that will remind you of a county fair prize winner. If you have any doubts of the quality of the peaches, use unthawed frozen peach slices, which are quite reliable, a very lightly processed product without any chemical preservatives or sweeteners. To peel fresh peaches, drop them into boiling water and cook for one minute. Drain them, rinse under cold water, and remove the loosened peels with a small sharp knife.

8 large (about 2 pounds) ripe free-stone peaches, peeled, pitted, and cut into ½-inch-thick slices (about 7½ cups)

4 tablespoons unbleached all-purpose flour, divided

½ cup liquid fruit juice concentrate or Fruit Juice Reduction (page 23)

2 tablespoons arrowroot

1 teaspoon ground ginger

1 teaspoon ground cinnamon

New-Fashioned Pie Dough (page 98)

Milk, for glazing

1   Position a rack in the center of the oven and preheat the oven to 350° F.

2   In a medium bowl, toss the peaches with *2 tablespoons* of the flour and set aside. In a small bowl, whisk the fruit juice concentrate with the *remaining* 2 tablespoons flour, arrowroot, ginger, and cinnamon and set aside.

3   On a lightly floured work surface, roll out the dough into a 14-inch circle about ⅛ inch thick. Transfer to a 10-inch pie plate, letting the excess dough hang over the sides. Pour the peaches into the pie plate, then pour the fruit juice concentrate mixture over the peaches. Fold the pastry overhang up over the fruit. Pleat the dough as necessary, leaving the center of the filling exposed. Brush the dough lightly with milk. Place on a baking sheet.

4   Bake until the crust is golden brown and the juices in the center of the pie are bubbling and look as thick as jam, 50 minutes to 1 hour. Cool for at least 45 minutes on a wire cake rack. Serve warm or at room temperature.

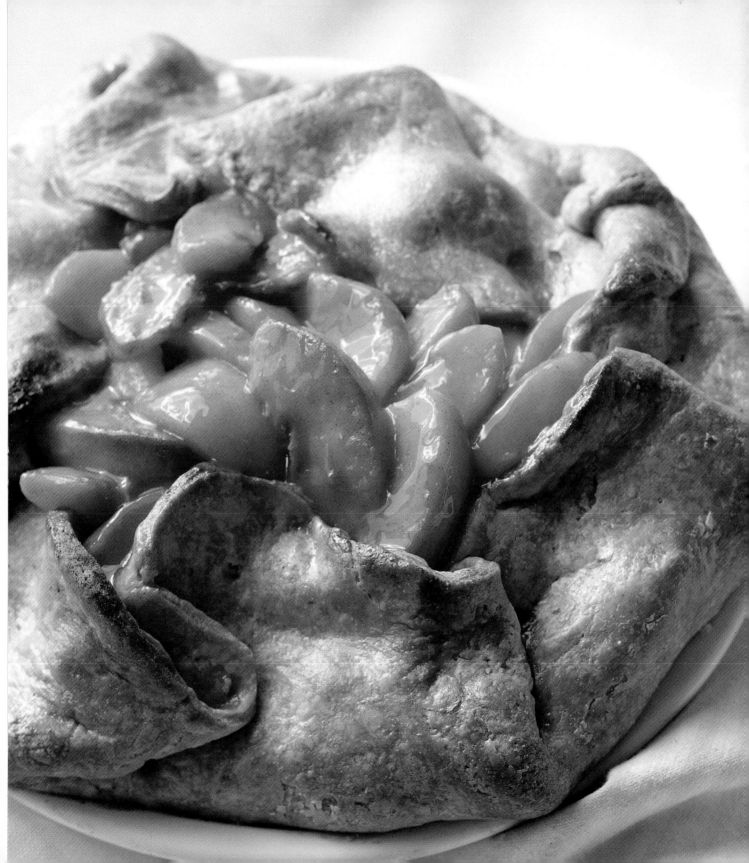

Pear Frangipane Tart

Makes 6 to 8 servings

Every year I look forward to making this seasonal treat when pears are at their peak. Bosc or Bartlett Pears are the best varieties to use, since they hold their shape during baking.

WHOLE WHEAT PASTRY

1¼ cups whole wheat pastry flour

¼ teaspoon salt

5 tablespoons unsalted butter, chilled, cut into ½-inch cubes

6 tablespoons ice water

PEAR-ALMOND FILLING

4 medium-size, firm-ripe cooking pears, such as Bosc or Bartlett

2 teaspoons fresh lemon juice

2 teaspoons unsalted butter, melted

¾ cup unblanched sliced almonds

1 tablespoon unbleached all-purpose flour

5 tablespoons unsalted butter, softened

⅓ cup liquid fruit juice concentrate or Fruit Juice Reduction (page 23)

1 large egg

1 To make the pastry: In a medium bowl, combine the flour and salt. Add the butter. Using a pastry blender or 2 forks, cut the butter into the flour until the mixture resembles coarse meal. Stirring with a fork, gradually add ice water just until the dough is moist enough to hold together when pinched between your thumb and forefinger. You may not need all of the water and the dough does not have to form a ball. Gather up the dough, flatten into a thick disk, and wrap in wax paper. Refrigerate until chilled, at least 1 hour or up to 1 day.

2 On a lightly floured work surface, roll out the dough into an 11-inch circle about ⅛ inch thick. (If the dough cracks, it may be too cold. Let stand at room temperature for 10 minutes and try rolling again.) Transfer to a 9-inch tart pan with a removable bottom. Press the dough into the corners to make a right angle. Trim the dough so it is even with the top of the pan. Prick the tart shell a few times with a fork. Cover with plastic wrap and put in the freezer for 15 minutes. Put the tart on a baking sheet.

3 Position a rack in the center of the oven and preheat the oven to 400° F.

4 To make the filling: Peel the pears, cut in half lengthwise, and core. Place a pear half on a cutting board, cut side down, and cut crosswise into ¼-inch-thick slices. Slide a metal spatula or wide knife under the pear half and transfer to the tart shell. Gently press down to fan out the pear slices. Repeat with the other pears, overlapping the pears in a circle in the tart shell. Brush the pears with lemon juice, then with melted butter.

5 In a food processor fitted with the metal blade or a blender, process the almonds with the flour until very finely ground. In a medium bowl, using a hand-held electric mixer set at medium speed, beat the butter with the fruit juice concentrate until combined. Beat in the almonds and the egg. Pour into the tart shell.

6 Bake for 10 minutes. Reduce the heat to 375° F. and bake until the filling is golden brown and the pears are tender when pierced with the tip of a sharp knife, 40 to 50 minutes longer. Cool completely on a wire cake rack. Remove the sides of the pan and serve.

Pear Frangipane Custard: Lightly spray the inside of a 9-inch quiche pan with nonstick spray. Arrange the pears in the pan, fan out the slices, and pour in the almond mixture. Bake in a preheated 350° F. oven until the top is golden brown and the pears are tender, about 40 minutes.

Apple-Cherry Cobbler

No Added Fat

Makes 6 servings

One of America's favorite homey desserts gets updated with a low-fat cobbler topping. This is a perfect choice for those on restricted-fat diets. You can use fresh or frozen cherries.

APPLE-CHERRY FILLING

1 cup liquid fruit juice concentrate or Fruit Juice Reduction (page 23)

2 tablespoons unbleached all-purpose flour

1 tablespoon fresh lemon juice

2 teaspoons ground cinnamon

1 teaspoon ground ginger

6 medium-size tart apples, such as Granny Smith, peeled, cored, and cut lengthwise into ½-inch-thick slices

2 cups (1 pound) bing cherries, pitted, or 12 ounces unthawed frozen sweet cherries

COBBLER

3 large egg whites

½ cup liquid fruit juice concentrate or Fruit Juice Reduction (page 23)

1 cup whole wheat pastry flour

⅓ cup nonfat dry milk

⅓ cup rolled old-fashioned oats

1 Position a rack in the center of the oven and preheat the oven to 425° F.

2 **To make the filling:** In a medium bowl, whisk the fruit juice concentrate, flour, lemon juice, cinnamon, and ginger until the flour is dissolved. Place the apples in an 8 x 11-inch baking dish, pour in the fruit juice concentrate mixture and toss. Bake until the apples are crisp-tender, about 20 minutes. Remove from the oven and stir in the cherries. Reduce the oven temperature to 350° F.

3 **To make the cobbler:** In a grease-free medium bowl, using a hand-held electric mixer set at high speed, beat the egg whites until soft peaks form. Add the fruit juice concentrate and beat until stiff peaks form.

4 In another medium bowl, combine the flour, dry milk, and oats. Add the egg whites. Using a rubber spatula, fold together gently to form a batter. It will deflate, but do not over-mix. Using a large spoon, drop 6 portions of the batter evenly over the fruit mixture.

5 Return the cobbler to the oven and bake until the topping is golden brown and a toothpick inserted in the center comes out clean, 20 to 25 minutes. Serve the cobbler warm.

Fresh Strawberry Tartlets

Egg Free

Makes 6 tartlets

The whipped cream–cream cheese filling used in these berry-topped tartlets is very easy and versatile, and you may find yourself literally whipping it up to use in your own impromptu pastry creations. The tart shells are baked completely before filling, using a traditional French baking technique of lining the dough with foil and weighting it down with dried beans or rice to discourage the sides of the dough from falling down during baking. Don't discard the used beans or rice: Store them in a jar for the next time you bake an empty pastry shell—they will last for at least a year in a cool, dry place.

Butter, for the pans

New Fashioned Pie Dough (page 98)

1 package (3 ounces) cream cheese, softened

1 cup heavy (whipping) cream, divided

⅓ cup liquid fruit juice concentrate or Fruit Juice Reduction (page 23)

¼ teaspoon vanilla extract

2 pints fresh strawberries, hulled

½ cup fruit-sweetened apricot spread

2 tablespoons water

1 Position a rack in the center of the oven and preheat to 400° F. Lightly butter six 4-inch tartlet pans with removable bottoms. Place the tartlet pans on a large baking sheet.

2 Cut the dough into 6 equal portions. Lightly knead each piece into a thick disk. On a lightly floured work surface, roll out one of the disks into a circle about 5½ inches in diameter and ⅛ inch thick. Transfer the dough to a tartlet pan, carefully pressing in the dough to create a right angle where the sides meet the bottom. Trim the excess dough flush with the top of the pan. Using a fork, prick the dough a few times. Line the inside of the pan with a piece of aluminum foil. Weight the foil with a handful of rice or dried beans. Place on a baking sheet. Repeat with the remaining dough.

3 Bake until the dough is set, about 10 minutes. Remove the foil and beans, and continue baking until the pastry is crisp and lightly browned, 5 to 8 minutes. Cool completely on the baking sheet. *(The shells can be prepared up to 1 day ahead, covered with plastic wrap and stored at room temperature.)*

4 In a medium bowl, using a handheld electric mixer set at low speed, beat the cream cheese with *¼ cup* of the heavy cream until smooth. Add the *remaining ¾ cup* heavy cream, the fruit juice concentrate, and vanilla. Increase the mixer speed to medium and beat just until the cream forms soft peaks. Do not overbeat or the mixture will separate. Spread evenly in the tartlet shells. Cover loosely with plastic wrap and refrigerate until the cream is somewhat firmed, at least 1 hour or up to 1 day.

5 Place a large strawberry, stem side down, in the center of each tart. Slice the remaining strawberries and arrange with the pointed ends facing the center in concentric circles.

6 In a small nonreactive saucepan over medium low heat, bring the apricot spread and water to a simmer, stirring constantly, then cook for 1 minute. Brush the berries with the glaze while it is still warm and liquid. Refrigerate the tartlets until ready to serve, no longer than 8 hours. Remove the sides of the pans just before serving.

Raspberry Tartlets: Arrange about ½ cup fresh raspberries, stem sides down, in concentric circles on each tartlet instead of strawberries.

Blueberry Tartlets: Sprinkle about ½ cup fresh blueberries on top of each tartlet instead of strawberries.

Lemon Meringue Tartlets

Whole Grain

Makes 8 tartlets

Lemon tartlets were the first "hit single" at Mäni's Bakery—they were the dessert that made people sit up and question, "This is sugar free?" Up to that point, I had been trying to make everything without dairy products, which was very limiting. After I loosened up and let milk and butter into the bakery, I realized that there are a lot of dietary preferences out there, and that quality ingredients are the first step to healthy eating. If your diet allows you a moderate amount of fat, here's a splurge dessert.

SWEET PASTRY CRUST

12 tablespoons (1½ sticks) unsalted butter, melted

5 tablespoons liquid fruit juice concentrate or Fruit Juice Reduction (page 23)

3 cups whole wheat pastry flour

LEMON FILLING

1⅓ cups liquid fruit juice concentrate or Fruit Juice Reduction (page 23)

4 large eggs

Grated zest of 1½ lemons

¼ cup fresh lemon juice

MERINGUE

3 large egg whites

¼ teaspoon cream of tartar

⅓ cup liquid fruit juice concentrate or Fruit Juice Reduction (page 23)

1 **To make the crust:** Position racks in the center and bottom third of the oven and preheat the oven to 400° F. Lightly butter eight 4-inch tartlet pans with removable bottoms.

2 In a medium bowl, whisk the melted butter and fruit juice concentrate until smooth. Place the flour in another medium bowl. Using a wooden spoon, stir in the butter mixture just until moistened and beginning to form large clumps. The dough will hold together when pinched with your thumb and forefinger. Do not overwork the dough. Gather the dough into a mass. Proceed right away—you must work with the dough while it is still warm.

3 Divide the dough into 8 portions and place each portion in a tartlet pan. Use your fingers to press the dough firmly and evenly into the pans. Press the pastry in where the sides meet the bottom to make a right angle, or the dough will be too

thick there. Prick the dough well with a fork. Place the tartlet pans on 2 baking sheets.

4 Place the sheets on the oven racks, staggered so the sheets are not directly above and below each other. Bake until the dough is set, about 10 minutes. Check once or twice during baking to be sure that the pastry isn't puffing up. If it is, prick it with a fork to deflate.

5 **To make the filling:** While the shells are baking, in a medium bowl, whisk the fruit juice concentrate, eggs, lemon zest, and lemon juice. Pour into a liquid measuring cup. When the crusts are set, pour the lemon filling into the crusts. This is easiest to do with the crusts still in the oven. Pull out the baking sheets on the oven racks a little and fill the crusts. Carefully slide the racks back in, trying to avoid spilling the filling. Immediately reduce the oven temperature to 350° F. Bake until the filling feels firm to the touch

and set in the centers, 20 to 25 minutes. Remove from the oven. Return the oven temperature to 400° F.

6 **To make the meringue:** In a grease-free medium bowl, using a handheld electric mixer set on high speed, beat the egg whites until foamy. Add the cream of tartar and beat until soft peaks form. Still beating, gradually add the fruit juice concentrate. Beat until stiff peaks form. Spread the meringue over the tartlets, being sure that it touches the crust and slightly overlaps it. (This will guard against shrinkage, which is a problem with all meringues but is even worse when liquid fruit concentrate is used instead of regular sugar.) Return to the oven and bake until the meringue is browned, 5 to 8 minutes. Cool completely on wire cake racks. Remove the sides of the pans and serve.

Pink Grapefruit Sorbet

Low Fat

Egg Free

Dairy Free

Makes about 1½ quarts, 6 to 8 servings

Sorbets deliver pure, undiluted fruit flavor without any dairy products, making them the ideal dessert for lactose-intolerant people. To obtain a smooth, icy texture, sorbets are made in an ice cream machine. Almost any citrus juice can be substituted for the pink grapefruit juice, but you will need to adjust the amount of fruit juice concentrate to taste. Remember that freezing dulls the tastebuds, so the fruit mixture must taste overly sweet before preparation in order to obtain the proper flavor at serving time.

3 cups fresh pink grapefruit juice

2 cups liquid fruit juice concentrate or Fruit Juice Reduction (page 23)

2 tablespoons fresh lemon juice

Grated zest of 1 grapefruit

1 In a medium nonreactive saucepan over low heat, cook the grapefruit juice, fruit juice concentrate, and lemon juice, whisking constantly, until the concentrate is dissolved. Do not bring to a simmer. Stir in the grapefruit zest. Transfer to a large bowl placed in a larger bowl of iced water. Let stand, stirring often, until the mixture is well chilled, about 20 minutes.

2 Pour the mixture into the container of an ice cream maker and freeze according to the manufacturer's instructions. Transfer the sorbet into a large airtight container. Cover, place in the freezer, and freeze until firm, at least 4 hours. Serve frozen.

Two-Berry Granita

Low Fat

Egg Free

Dairy Free

Makes about 1 quart, 4 to 6 servings

Granitas are perhaps the simplest of all frozen desserts to make since they don't require an ice cream maker. They have a coarse grainy texture that can be very refreshing on a hot summer afternoon. It takes a couple of hours for the granita to freeze, but the freezer does most of the work.

2 cups (12 ounces) fresh raspberries

2 cups (16 ounces) fresh blueberries

1¼ cups liquid fruit juice concentrate or Fruit Juice Reduction (page 23)

2 tablespoons fresh lemon juice

1 Place a 9-inch square metal pan and a large metal spoon in the freezer and freeze until well chilled, about 30 minutes.

2 In a food processor fitted with the metal blade, puree the raspberries, blueberries, fruit juice concentrate, and lemon juice. Transfer to the metal pan and spread evenly. Leave the metal spoon in the pan.

3 Freeze until the edges of the puree are semifirm and icy, about 1 hour. Use the spoon to break up the icy areas and stir them into the center of the puree. Repeat the freezing and stirring procedure about every 30 minutes until the mixture is frozen, 2 to 2½ hours. Serve immediately. *(If the granita freezes too hard to scoop, chop it into chunks and pulse in a food processor fitted with the metal blade until broken up.)*

Strawberry Custard Cups

Low Fat

Makes 4 servings

I love strawberries, and these not-too-sweet custard cups make a cool finish to a warm-weather meal. You may use either reduced-fat or regular sour cream, but do not use the nonfat version.

⅓ cup liquid fruit juice concentrate or Fruit Juice Reduction (page 23)

1 tablespoon cornstarch

1 cup reduced-fat sour cream

2 large egg whites

1 teaspoon vanilla extract

1 pint (about 15) strawberries, hulled

½ cup fruit-sweetened apricot spread

2 tablespoons water

1 Preheat the oven to 350° F.

2 In a medium bowl, whisk the fruit juice concentrate and cornstarch until the cornstarch is dissolved. Whisk in the sour cream, egg whites and vanilla. Pour into 4 ungreased ½-cup custard cups or ramekins. Place the cups on a baking sheet.

3 Bake until the custards seem almost set in the center when jiggled, about 12 minutes. Cool completely.

4 Place a single large strawberry, stem side down, in the center of each custard. Thinly slice the remaining berries. Surround each strawberry with over-lapping sliced berries, pointed ends facing the center.

5 In a small saucepan over low heat, bring the apricot spread and water to a simmer. Cook for 1 minute. Brush the berries with the apricot glaze. Refrigerate until ready to serve.

Mäni's Sugar-Free Truffles

Egg Free

Makes about 24 truffles

At Mäni's Bakery, we make these outrageous indulgences in two versions: dairy-free with soy milk and dairy with heavy cream. It is impossible to say which is better. See the variation following the recipe for dairy-free truffles. Don't worry if your dipped truffles have a rough surface; any flaws will be disguised by rolling in a coating of your choice. Dutch-process cocoa powder has been harmlessly alkalized, reducing the acidity of the cocoa and giving it a mellower taste; it's a better choice than regular cocoa for rolling truffles. This is a fun project to do with a friend—it always reminds me of the time Lucy and Ethel worked in the chocolate factory, eating almost as many chocolates as they dipped!

FILLING

⅔ cup heavy (whipping) cream

2⅓ cups (14 ounces) malt-sweetened semisweet chocolate chips

DIPPING AND ROLLING

1½ cups (9 ounces) malt-sweetened semisweet chocolate chips

1½ teaspoons vegetable oil

½ cup cocoa powder, preferably Dutch process

1 **To make the filling:** In a medium saucepan, heat the cream over low heat until small bubbles appear around the edges. Remove the saucepan from the heat.

2 Place the chocolate chips in a medium bowl. Pour in the hot cream and let stand for 1 minute. Whisk gently until the chips are completely melted and the mixture is smooth. Transfer to a 7 x 11-inch baking pan and let stand at cool room temperature until firm, at least 4 hours. The filling mixture can also be refrigerated, but don't refrigerate it until it is rock hard, just until firm enough to roll into balls.

3 **To roll and dip the truffles:** Line a baking sheet with wax paper. Using a melon baller or a dessert spoon, scoop up the chocolate filling, roll between your palms to form 1-inch balls, and place on the baking sheet. Freeze the balls until ready to dip.

4 In the top part of a double boiler set over very hot, but not simmering, water, melt the chocolate chips and oil, stirring occasionally, until smooth.

5 It is best to have a friend help you coat the truffles, as one person's hands will be covered in chocolate from the dipping. Line another baking sheet with wax or parchment paper. Place the cocoa powder in a small, shallow dish. Place the ingredients in a line in front of you in the following order: the baking sheet with the chocolate balls, the melted chocolate, the dish of cocoa powder, and the clean baking sheet.

6 Pick up a chocolate ball and place it in the palm of your hand. Spoon about 1 tablespoon of melted chocolate over the ball. Roll the ball between your palms, lightly but completely coating the ball in chocolate. (This will give you a thinner shell than dipping the ball in the chocolate and fishing it out, and to my mind it's much simpler.) Transfer the dipped truffle to the cocoa and roll to coat completely, then transfer to the clean baking sheet. If the truffle seems too soft to place on the baking sheet, refrigerate the truffle in the dish of cocoa until it firms up.

Recipe continues on page 124.

7 Refrigerate the coated truffles until the chocolate coating is hard, about 10 minutes. Transfer the truffles to an airtight container. *(Store, refrigerated, for up to 5 days.)* Serve the truffles slightly chilled.

Soy Milk Truffles:
Substitute ⅔ cup sweetened soy milk for the heavy cream. Do not let the soy milk reach the simmering point; cook just until very hot. Substitute 2 cups (12 ounces) chocolate chips and 2 ounces finely chopped unsweetened chocolate for the 2⅓ cups chocolate chips in the recipe. The unsweetened chocolate helps balance the sweet flavor of the soy milk.

Almond Truffles: In a preheated 350° F. oven, bake 1½ cups (6 ounces) sliced almonds, stirring often, until lightly toasted and fragrant, 8 to 10 minutes. Cool completely. In a food processor fitted with the metal blade or using a large sharp knife, chop the almonds until very fine. Roll the dipped truffles in the almonds instead of cocoa powder. Pecans or walnuts may also be used.

Coconut Truffles: In a preheated 350° F. oven, bake 1 cup unsweetened dessicated coconut, stirring occasionally, until lightly toasted, 8 to 10 minutes. Roll the dipped truffles in the toasted coconut instead of the cocoa powder.

Nutritional Analysis by Recipe

Almond Jewel Cookies
Per Serving (1 cookie):
Calories: 90
   8% from protein,
   64% from carbohydrate,
   28% from fat
Protein: 2 g
Carbohydrate: 15 g
Fat: 3 g
Cholesterol: 0 mg
Sodium: 45 g

Almond Shortbread
Per Serving (1 piece):
Calories: 438
   7% from protein,
   31% from carbohydrate,
   62% from fat
Protein: 7 g
Carbohydrate: 35 g
Fat: 31 g
Cholesterol: 55 mg
Sodium: 6 g

**Apple-Blueberry
Double Crust Pie**
Per Serving (1 slice):
Calories: 343
   4% from protein,
   58% from carbohydrate,
   38% from fat
Protein: 4 g
Carbohydrate: 51 g
Fat: 15 g
Cholesterol: 39 mg
Sodium: 84 g

Apple-Cherry Cobbler
Per Serving (1 piece):
Calories: 403
   10% from protein,
   86% from carbohydrate,
   4% from fat
Protein: 10 g
Carbohydrate: 90 g
Fat: 2 g
Cholesterol: 1 mg
Sodium: 91 g

**Apple–Pecan
Praline Tart**
Per Serving (1 tart):
Calories: 373
   4% from protein,
   43% from carbohydrate,
   54% from fat

Protein: 4 g
Carbohydrate: 41 g
Fat: 23 g
Cholesterol: 43 mg
Sodium: 83 g

**Applesauce-Currant
Cookies**
Per Serving (1 cookie):
Calories: 108
   11% from protein,
   71% from carbohydrate,
   18% from fat
Protein: 3 g
Carbohydrate: 19 g
Fat: 2 g
Cholesterol: 0 mg
Sodium: 81 g

**Apple Streusel
Coffeecake**
Per Serving (1 piece):
Calories: 282
   9% from protein,
   71% from carbohydrate,
   19% from fat
Protein: 7 g
Carbohydrate: 50 g
Fat: 6 g
Cholesterol: 62 mg
Sodium: 263 g

**Apple Tart with Yogurt
Custard in Walnut-Oat
Crust (with crust)**
Per Serving (1 piece):
Calories: 235
   11% from protein,
   55% from carbohydrate,
   33% from fat
Protein: 7 g
Carbohydrate: 33 g
Fat: 9 g
Cholesterol: 54 mg
Sodium: 94 g

**Apple Tart with Yogurt
Custard in Walnut-Oat
Crust (without crust)**
Per Serving (1 piece):
Calories: 85
   15% from protein,
   70% from carbohydrate,
   15% from fat
Protein: 3 g
Carbohydrate: 15 g

Fat: 1 g
Cholesterol: 54 mg
Sodium: 40 g

Apple Turnovers
Per Serving (1 turnover):
Calories: 478
   5% from protein,
   52% from carbohydrate,
   43% from fat
Protein: 6 g
Carbohydrate: 64 g
Fat: 24 g
Cholesterol: 62 mg
Sodium: 162 g

**Baked Apples with
Maple Pecan Crust**
Per Serving (1 apple):
Calories: 134
   2% from protein,
   60% from carbohydrate,
   38% from fat
Protein: 1 g
Carbohydrate: 22 g
Fat: 6 g
Cholesterol: 3 mg
Sodium: 3 g

**Banana Layer Cake
with Cream Cheese
Frosting**
Per Serving (1 slice):
Calories: 487
   6% from protein,
   40% from carbohydrate,
   54% from fat
Protein: 8 g
Carbohydrate: 50 g
Fat: 30 g
Cholesterol: 77 mg
Sodium: 239 g

Banana-Nut Pancakes
Per Serving (1 pancake):
Calories: 147
   11% from protein,
   48% from carbohydrate,
   41% from fat
Protein: 4 g
Carbohydrate: 18 g
Fat: 7 g
Cholesterol: 30 mg
Sodium: 85 g

Banana-Pecan Scones
Per Serving (1 scone):
Calories: 337
   6% from protein,
   58% from carbohydrates,
   36% from fat
Protein: 5 g
Carbohydrates: 50 g
Fat: 14 g
Cholesterol: l6 mg
Sodium: 154 g

Banana-Walnut Muffins
Per Serving (1 muffin):
Calories: 187
   10% from protein,
   61% from carbohydrate,
   29% from fat
Protein: 5 g
Carbohydrate: 30 g
Fat: 7 g
Cholesterol: 18 mg
Sodium: 166 g

Barley-Currant Scones
Per Serving (1 scone):
Calories: 230
   8% from protein,
   61% from carbohydrate,
   32% from fat
Protein: 5 g
Carbohydrate: 36 g
Fat: 8 g
Cholesterol: 40 mg
Sodium: 152 g

**Blackberry
Upside-Down Cake**
Per Serving (1 slice):
Calories: 261
   8% from protein,
   52% from carbohydrate,
   40% from fat
Protein: 5 g
Carbohydrate: 34 g
Fat: 12 g
Cholesterol: less than 1 mg
Sodium: 143 g

**Black Forest Bundt
Cake**
Per Serving (1 slice):
Calories: 272
   12% from protein,
   70% from carbohydrate,
   18% from fat

Protein: 8 g
Carbohydrate: 48 g
Fat: 6 g
Cholesterol: 36 mg
Sodium: 281 g

Blood Orange Sherbet
Per Serving (about ¾ cup):
Calories: 126
   11% from protein,
   81% from carbohydrate,
   8% from fat
Protein: 3 g
Carbohydrate: 26 g
Fat: 1 g
Cholesterol: 4 mg
Sodium: 52 g

Blueberry Buttermilk Pancakes
Per Serving (1 pancake):
Calories: 113
   18% from protein,
   70% from carbohydrate,
   12% from fat
Protein: 5 g
Carbohydrate: 20 g
Fat: 2 g
Cholesterol: 37 mg
Sodium: 140 g

Blueberry Corn Muffins
Per Serving (1 muffin):
Calories: 227
   5% from protein,
   58% from carbohydrate,
   33% from fat
Protein: 5 g
Carbohydrate: 33 g
Fat: 8 g
Cholesterol: 28 mg
Sodium: 243 g

Blueberry–Oat Bran Muffins
Per Serving (1 muffin):
Calories: 110
   10% from protein,
   58% from carbohydrate,
   32% from fat
Protein: 3 g
Carbohydrate: 17 g
Fat: 4 g
Cholesterol: 0 mg
Sodium: 92 g

Butter Spritz Cookies
Per Serving (1 cookie):
Calories: 56

4% from protein,
47% from carbohydrate,
49% from fat
Protein: 1 g
Carbohydrate: 7 g
Fat: 3 g
Cholesterol: 17 mg
Sodium: 14 g

Carrot-Pineapple Muffins
Per Serving (1 muffin):
Calories: 160
   13% from protein,
   84% from carbohydrate,
   3% from fat
Protein: 5 g
Carbohydrate: 35 g
Fat: less than 1 g
Cholesterol: less than 1 mg
Sodium: 127 g

Chocolate Chip and Pecan Cookies
Per Serving (1 cookie):
Calories: 183
   4% from protein,
   50% from carbohydrate,
   46% from fat
Protein: 2 g
Carbohydrate: 23 g
Fat: 10 g
Cholesterol: 0 mg
Sodium: 124 g

Chocolate-dipped Barley Cookies
Per Serving (1 cookie):
Calories: 152
   3% from protein,
   53% from carbohydrate,
   44% from fat
Protein: 1 g
Carbohydrate: 21 g
Fat: 8 g
Cholesterol: 0 mg
Sodium: 53 g

Chocolate Raspberry Fortress Cake
Per Serving (1 slice):
Calories: 469
   6% from protein,
   40% from carbohydrate,
   54% from fat
Protein: 8 g
Carbohydrate: 46 g
Fat: 28 g
Cholesterol: 137 mg
Sodium: 329 g

Chocolate Truffle Heart Cookies
Per Serving (1 cookie):
Calories: 314
   3% from protein,
   49% from carbohydrate,
   48% from fat
Protein: 3 g
Carbohydrate: 39 g
Fat: 17 g
Cholesterol: 46 mg
Sodium: 94 g

Chocolate-Walnut Muffins
Per Serving (1 muffin):
Calories: 205
   10% from protein,
   46% from carbohydrate,
   44% from fat
Protein: 5 g
Carbohydrate: 24 g
Fat: 10 g
Cholesterol: 0 mg
Sodium: 179 g

Chunky Carrot Cake
Per Serving (1 slice):
Calories: 346
   6% from protein,
   43% from carbohydrate,
   51% from fat
Protein: 5 g
Carbohydrate: 39 g
Fat: 20 g
Cholesterol: 0 mg
Sodium: 135 g

Coconut Macaroons
Per Serving (1 macaroon):
Calories: 110
   5% from protein,
   57% from carbohydrate,
   38% from fat
Protein: 1 g
Carbohydrate: 16 g
Fat: 5 g
Cholesterol: 0 mg
Sodium: 71 g

Cranberry-Walnut Scones
Per Serving (1 scone):
Calories: 237
   7% from protein,
   53% from carbohydrate,
   40% from fat
Protein: 4 g
Carbohydrate: 32 g
Fat: 11 g
Cholesterol: 16 mg
Sodium: 93 g

Deep Dark Brownies
Per Serving (1 brownie):
Calories: 306
   5% from protein,
   39% from carbohydrate,
   56% from fat
Protein: 4 g
Carbohydrate: 31 g
Fat: 19 g
Cholesterol: 63 mg
Sodium: 79 g

Faux-Nuts
Per Serving (1 faux-nut):
Calories: 275
   9% from protein,
   70% from carbohydrate,
   21% from fat
Protein: 6 g
Carbohydrate: 49 g
Fat: 6 g
Cholesterol: 53 mg
Sodium: 211 g

Fresh Strawberry Tartlets
Per Serving (1 tart):
Calories: 537
   4% from protein,
   38% from carbohydrate,
   58% from fat
Protein: 6 g
Carbohydrate: 52 g
Fat: 36 g
Cholesterol: 112 mg
Sodium: 166 g

Fresh Strawberry Scones
Per Serving (1 scone):
Calories: 232
   5% from protein,
   72% from carbohydrate,
   23% from fat
Protein: 3 g
Carbohydrate: 42 g
Fat: 6 g
Cholesterol: 16 mg
Sodium: 154 g

Ginger Happy Face Cookies
Per Serving (1 cookie):
Calories: 126
   7% from protein,
   76% from carbohydrate,
   17% from fat
Protein: 2 g
Carbohydrate: 25 g
Fat: 2 g
Cholesterol: 6 mg
Sodium: 84 g

Granola Triple Oat Cookie
Per Serving (1 cookie):
Calories: 147
    7% from protein,
    48% from carbohydrate,
    45% from fat
Protein: 3 g
Carbohydrate: 18 g
Fat: 7 g
Cholesterol: 0 mg
Sodium: 80 g

Hollywood Cheesecake
Per Serving (1 slice):
Calories: 451
    8% from protein,
    23% from carbohydrate,
    69% from fat
Protein: 9 g
Carbohydrate: 27 g
Fat: 35 g
Cholesterol: 169 mg
Sodium: 311 g

Huckleberry-Apple Muffins
Per Serving (1 muffin):
Calories: 241
    8% from protein,
    60% from carbohydrate,
    32% from fat
Protein: 5 g
Carbohydrate: 37 g
Fat: 9 g
Cholesterol: 62 mg
Sodium: 137 g

Lemon Meringue Tartlets
Per Serving (1 tart):
Calories: 478
    9% from protein,
    53% from carbohydrate,
    38% from fat
Protein: 11 g
Carbohydrate: 65 g
Fat: 20 g
Cholesterol: 151 mg
Sodium: 64 g

Lemon Poppy Gems
Per Serving (1 cookie):
Calories: 76
    8% from protein,
    74% from carbohydrate,
    19% from fat
Protein: 2 g
Carbohydrate: 14 g
Fat: 2 g
Cholesterol: 0 mg
Sodium: 47 g

Mäni's Sugar-Free Truffles (with cream, rolled in cocoa)
Per Serving (1 truffle):
Calories: 169
    2% from protein,
    45% from carbohydrate,
    54% from fat
Protein: 1 g
Carbohydrate: 19 g
Fat: 10 g
Cholesterol: 9 mg
Sodium: 5 g

Mäni's Sugar-Free Truffles (with cream, rolled in almonds)
Per Serving (1 truffle):
Calories: 201
    3% from protein,
    38% from carbohydrate,
    59% from fat
Protein: 2 g
Carbohydrate: 20 g
Fat: 14 g
Cholesterol: 9 mg
Sodium: 5 g

Mäni's Sugar-Free Truffles (with cream, rolled in coconut)
Per Serving (1 truffle):
Calories: 179
    1% from protein,
    44% from carbohydrate,
    56% from fat
Protein: less than 1 g
Carbohydrate: 20 g
Fat: 11 g
Cholesterol: 9 mg
Sodium: 14 g

Mäni's Sugar-Free Truffles (with soy milk, rolled in cocoa)
Per Serving (1 truffle):
Calories: 149
    2% from protein,
    51% from carbohydrate,
    47% from fat
Protein: 1 g
Carbohydrate: 19 g
Fat: 8 g
Cholesterol: 0 mg
Sodium: 3 g

Mäni's Sugar-Free Truffles (with soy milk, rolled in almonds)
Per Serving (1 truffle):
Calories: 180
    3% from protein,
    42% from carbohydrate,
    55% from fat
Protein: 2 g
Carbohydrate: 20 g
Fat: 11 g
Cholesterol: 0 mg
Sodium: 3 g

Mäni's Sugar-Free Truffles (with soy milk, rolled in coconut)
Per Serving (1 truffle):
Calories: 158
    1% from protein,
    49% from carbohydrate,
    50% from fat
Protein: less than 1 g
Carbohydrate: 20 g
Fat: 9 g
Cholesterol: 0 mg
Sodium: 13 g

Mocha Almond Cake
Per Serving (1 slice):
Calories: 664
    6% from protein,
    23% from carbohydrate,
    72% from fat
Protein: 10 g
Carbohydrate: 39 g
Fat: 54 g
Cholesterol: 216 mg
Sodium: 252 g

Modern Mini Fruitcakes
Per Serving (½-inch slice):
Calories: 63
    10% from protein,
    75% from carbohydrate,
    15% from fat
Protein: 2 g
Carbohydrate: 12 g
Fat: 1 g
Cholesterol: 12 mg
Sodium: 50 g

New-Fashioned Pie Dough
Per Serving (without filling):
Calories: 181
    5% from protein,
    38% from carbohydrate,
    57% from fat
Protein: 2 g
Carbohydrate: 18 g

Fat: 12 g
Cholesterol: 31 mg
Sodium: 79 g

Oil-Free Cornmeal Muffins
Per Serving (1 muffin):
Calories: 174
    12% from protein,
    78% from carbohydrate,
    10% from fat
Protein: 5 g
Carbohydrate: 34 g
Fat: 2 g
Cholesterol: 54 mg
Sodium: 176 g

Peach Foldover Pie
Per Serving (1 slice):
Calories: 270
    5% from protein,
    57% from carbohydrate,
    38% from fat
Protein: 3 g
Carbohydrate: 40 g
Fat: 12 g
Cholesterol: 31 mg
Sodium: 81 g

Peach–Poppy Seed Muffins
Per Serving (1 muffin):
Calories: 158
    14% from protein,
    80% from carbohydrate,
    6% from fat
Protein: 6 g
Carbohydrate: 33 g
Fat: 1 g
Cholesterol: less than 1 mg
Sodium: 142 g

Pear Frangipane Tart (with crust)
Per Serving (1 slice):
Calories: 262
    6% from protein,
    39% from carbohydrate,
    56% from fat
Protein: 4 g
Carbohydrate: 26 g
Fat: 17 g
Cholesterol: 52 mg
Sodium: 58 g

Pear Frangipane Tart (without crust)
Per Serving (1 slice):
Calories: 158
    6% from protein,
    35% from carbohydrate,
    59% from fat

Protein: 2 g
Carbohydrate: 15 g
Fat: 11 g
Cholesterol: 37 mg
Sodium: 4 g

Pineapple Frozen Yogurt
Per Serving (about ¾ cup):
Calories: 229
    13% from protein,
    86% from carbohydrate,
    1% from fat
Protein: 7 g
Carbohydrate: 50 g
Fat: less than 1 g
Cholesterol: 2 mg
Sodium: 93 g

Pink Grapefruit Sorbet
Per Serving (about ¾ cup):
Calories: 157
    1% from protein,
    98% from carbohydrate,
    1% from fat
Protein: 1 g
Carbohydrate: 40 g
Fat: less than 1 g
Cholesterol: 0 mg
Sodium: 11 g

Pumpkin-Yam Pie (with crust)
Per Serving (1 slice):
Calories: 339
    11% from protein,
    51% from carbohydrate,
    39% from fat
Protein: 9 g
Carbohydrate: 45 g
Fat: 15 g
Cholesterol: 31 mg
Sodium: 156 g

Pumpkin-Yam Pie (without crust)
Per Serving (1 slice):
Calories: 158
    16% from protein,
    65% from carbohydrate,
    19% from fat
Protein: 7 g
Carbohydrate: 27 g
Fat: 3 g
Cholesterol: 0 mg
Sodium: 77 g

Raisin Bran Muffins
Per Serving (1 muffin):
Calories: 142

9% from protein,
71% from carbohydrate,
21% from fat
Protein: 3 g
Carbohydrate: 27 g
Fat: 4 g
Cholesterol: less than 1 mg
Sodium: 108 g

Raspberry Linzer Cookies
Per Serving (1 cookie):
Calories: 307
    6% from protein,
    77% from carbohydrate,
    17% from fat
Protein: 5 g
Carbohydrate: 77 g
Fat: 6 g
Cholesterol: 0 mg
Sodium: 136 g

Raspberry–Oat Flour Muffins
Per Serving (1 muffin):
Calories: 156
    9% from protein,
    47% from carbohydrate,
    44% from fat
Protein: 4 g
Carbohydrate: 18 g
Fat: 8 g
Cholesterol: 51 mg
Sodium: 140 g

Red-Hot Peanut Butter Cookies
Per Serving (1 cookie):
Calories: 96
    13% from protein,
    38% from carbohydrate,
    48% from fat
Protein: 3 g
Carbohydrate: 10 g
Fat: 5 g
Cholesterol: 0 mg
Sodium: 95 g

Southern-style Cornmeal Waffles
Per Serving (1 waffle):
Calories: 136
    10% from protein,
    42% from carbohydrate,
    47% from fat
Protein: 4 g
Carbohydrate: 14 g
Fat: 7 g
Cholesterol: 36 mg
Sodium: 126 g

Sticky Pecan-Raisin Buns
Per Serving (1 bun):
Calories: 442
    7% from protein,
    53% from carbohydrate,
    41% from fat
Protein: 8 g
Carbohydrate: 60 g
Fat: 21 g
Cholesterol: 30 mg
Sodium: 147 g

Strawberry-Banana Ice Milk
Per Serving (about ¾ cup):
Calories: 192
    10% from protein,
    83% from carbohydrate,
    7% from fat
Protein: 5 g
Carbohydrate: 41 g
Fat: 2 g
Cholesterol: 5 mg
Sodium: 69 g

Strawberry Custard Cups
Per Serving (1 slice):
Calories: 189
    8% from protein,
    73% from carbohydrate,
    19% from fat
Protein: 4 g
Carbohydrate: 36 g
Fat: 4 g
Cholesterol: 19 mg
Sodium: 126 g

Strawberry Shortcakes with Mäni's Special Strawberry Sauce
Per Serving (1 shortcake with fruit and sauce):
Calories: 473
    5% from protein,
    55% from carbohydrate,
    40% from fat
Protein: 6 g
Carbohydrate: 66 g
Fat: 22 g
Cholesterol: 70 mg
Sodium: 316 g

Tropical Fruit Mousse Parfaits
Per Serving (1 parfait):
Calories: 259
    29% from protein,
    37% from carbohydrate,
    34% from fat

Protein: 20 g
Carbohydrate: 26 g
Fat: 10 g
Cholesterol: 0 mg
Sodium: 41 g

Two-Berry Granita
Per Serving (about ⅔ cup):
Calories: 161
    2% from protein,
    95% from carbohydrate,
    3% from fat
Protein: 1 g
Carbohydrate: 40 g
Fat: less than 1 g
Cholesterol: 0 mg
Sodium: 12 g

Vanilla Bean Ice Milk
Per Serving (about ¾ cup):
Calories: 141
    11% from protein,
    80% from carbohydrate,
    8% from fat
Protein: 4 g
Carbohydrate: 28 g
Fat: 1 g
Cholesterol: 5 mg
Sodium: 68 g

Washington State Blackberry Muffins
Per Serving (1 muffin):
Calories: 131
    9% from protein,
    64% from carbohydrate,
    27% from fat
Protein: 3 g
Carbohydrate: 21 g
Fat: 4 g
Cholesterol: 28 mg
Sodium: 111 g

Index

A

Almonds
Almond Jewel Cookies, 69
Almond Shortbread, 74
Almond Truffles, 124
Mocha Almond Cake, 92, 94
Pear Frangipane Custard, 104
Pear Frangipane Tart, 104

Apples
Apple-Blueberry Double Crust Pie, 106
Apple-Cherry Cobbler, 108
Apple–Pecan Praline Tart, 102
Apple Streusel Coffee Cake, 30
Apple Tart, 103
Apple Turnovers, 99
Apple-Yogurt Custard, 103
Baked Apples with Maple-Pecan Crust, 32
Huckleberry-Apple Muffins, 50
juice concentrate, 16, 17
Applesauce-Currant Cookies, 68

B

Baked Apples with Maple-Pecan Crust, 32

Bananas
Banana Layer Cake, 83
Banana-Nut Pancakes, 34
Banana-Pecan Scones, 37
Banana-Walnut Muffins, 56
Faux-Nuts, 28
Strawberry-Banana Ice Milk, 118

Barley
Barley-Currant Scones, 41
Chocolate-dipped Barley Cookies, 64

Blackberries
Blackberry Upside-Down Cake, 84
Washington State Blackberry Muffins, 51
Black Forest Bundt Cake, 82
Blood Orange Sherbet, 119

Blueberries
Apple-Blueberry Double Crust Pie, 106

Blueberry Buttermilk Pancakes, 33
Blueberry Corn Muffins, 45
Blueberry–Oat Bran Muffins, 49
Blueberry Tartlets, 110
Two-Berry Granita, 120

Bran
about, 21
Blueberry–Oat Bran Muffins, 49
Raisin Bran Muffins, 57
Brownies, Deep Dark, 62
Buns, Sticky Pecan-Raisin, 26
Butter Spritz Cookies, 70

C

Cakes
about, 79–81
Banana Layer Cake, 83
Blackberry Upside-Down Cake, 84
Black Forest Bundt Cake, 82
Chocolate Raspberry Fortress Cake, 86–87
Chunky Carrot Cake, 91
Hollywood Cheesecake, 90
Mocha Almond Cake, 92, 94
Modern Mini Fruitcakes, 88
Strawberry Shortcakes, 95

Carrots
Carrot-Pineapple Muffins, 54
Chunky Carrot Cake, 91
Cheesecake, Hollywood, 90

Cherries
Apple-Cherry Cobbler, 108
Black Forest Bundt Cake, 82

Chocolate
Black Forest Bundt Cake, 82
chips, 22
Chocolate Chip and Pecan Cookies, 61
Chocolate-dipped Barley Cookies, 64
Chocolate-dipped Faux-Nuts, 28
Chocolate Raspberry Fortress Cake, 86–87
Chocolate Truffle Heart Cookies, 66
Chocolate-Walnut Muffins, 46

Chocolate-Walnut Topping, 90
Deep Dark Brownies, 62
Sugar-Free Truffles, 122, 124
Chunky Carrot Cake, 91
Cobbler, Apple-Cherry, 108
Coconut Macaroons, 71
Coconut Truffles, 124
Coffee Cake, Apple Streusel, 30

Cookies
about, 59–60
Almond Jewel Cookies, 69
Almond Shortbread, 74
Applesauce-Currant Cookies, 68
Butter Spritz Cookies, 70
Chocolate Chip and Pecan Cookies, 61
Chocolate-dipped Barley Cookies, 64
Chocolate Truffle Heart Cookies, 66
Coconut Macaroons, 71
Deep Dark Brownies, 62
Ginger Happy Face Cookies, 75
Granola Triple Oat Cookies, 65
Lemon Poppy Gems, 77
Raspberry Linzer Cookies, 72
Red Hot Peanut Butter Cookies, 76

Cornmeal
Blueberry Corn Muffins, 45
Oil-Free Cornmeal Muffins, 48
Southern-style Cornmeal Waffles, 29
Cranberry-Walnut Scones, 38
Cream Cheese Frosting, 83

Currants
Applesauce-Currant Cookies, 68
Barley-Currant Scones, 41

Custards
Apple-Yogurt Custard, 103
Pear Frangipane Custard, 104
Strawberry Custard Cups, 121

D

Dairy-free recipes
Almond Jewel Cookies, 69
Apple-Blueberry Double Crust Pie, 106
Applesauce-Currant Cookies, 68
Banana-Nut Pancakes, 34
Barley-Currant Scones, 41
Blueberry–Oat Bran Muffins, 49
Chocolate Chip and Pecan Cookies, 61
Chocolate-dipped Barley Cookies, 64
Chocolate-Walnut Muffins, 46
Chunky Carrot Cake, 91
Granola Triple Oat Cookies, 65
Lemon Poppy Gems, 77
Pink Grapefruit Sorbet, 120
Pumpkin-Yam Pie, 107
Raspberry Linzer Cookies, 72
Red Hot Peanut Butter Cookies, 76
Tropical Fruit Mousse Parfait, 115
Two-Berry Granita, 120
Deep Dark Brownies, 62
Double Crust New-Fashioned Pie Dough, 98

E

Egg-free recipes
Almond Jewel Cookies, 69
Almond Shortbread, 74
Apple-Blueberry Double Crust Pie, 106
Apple–Pecan Praline Tart, 102
Apple Turnovers, 99
Baked Apples with Maple-Pecan Crust, 32
Banana-Pecan Scones, 37
Blood Orange Sherbet, 119
Blueberry–Oat Bran Muffins, 49
Chocolate Chip and Pecan Cookies, 61
Chocolate-dipped Barley

Cookies, 64
Chocolate-Walnut
  Muffins, 46
Chunky Carrot Cake, 91
Cranberry-Walnut
  Scones, 38
Fresh Strawberry Scones,
  40
Fresh Strawberry Tartlets,
  110
Ginger Happy Face
  Cookies, 75
Granola Triple Oat
  Cookies, 65
Lemon Poppy Gems, 77
New-Fashioned Pie
  Dough, 98
Peach Foldover Pie, 100
Pineapple Frozen Yogurt,
  119
Pink Grapefruit Sorbet,
  120
Pumpkin-Yam Pie, 107
Raisin Bran Muffins, 57
Raspberry Linzer
  Cookies, 72
Red Hot Peanut Butter
  Cookies, 76
Strawberry-Banana Ice
  Milk, 118
Strawberry Shortcakes, 95
Sticky Pecan-Raisin Buns,
  26
Sugar-Free Truffles, 122,
  124
Two-Berry Granita, 120
Vanilla Bean Ice Milk, 116

F
Faux-Nuts, 28
Flour, 18–20
Fresh Strawberry Scones, 40
Fresh Strawberry Tartlets,
  110
Frozen Yogurt, Pineapple,
  119
Fruit. *See also individual
  fruits*
Fruit Glaze Topping, 90
Fruit Juice Reduction, 23
Fruit Sweet, 16
juice, unsweetened
  organic, 17
juice concentrate, 16–17
Modern Mini Fruitcakes,
  88
purees, 21
spreads, fruit-sweetened,
  21–22
Tropical Fruit Mousse
  Parfait, 115

G
Ginger Happy Face Cookies,
  75
Granita, Two-Berry, 120
Granola Triple Oat
  Cookies, 65
Grapefruit Sorbet, Pink,
  120
Grape juice concentrate,
  16, 17

H
Hollywood Cheesecake, 90
Huckleberry-Apple
  Muffins, 50

I
Ice milk
  Strawberry-Banana Ice
    Milk, 118
  Vanilla Bean Ice Milk, 116

L
Lemon Meringue Tartlets,
  111
Lemon Poppy Gems, 77
Low-fat recipes. *See also*
  "No added fat" recipes
  Applesauce-Currant
    Cookies, 68
  Apple Streusel Coffee
    Cake, 30
  Baked Apples with
    Maple-Pecan Crust, 32
  Black Forest Bundt Cake, 82
  Blood Orange Sherbet, 119
  Blueberry Buttermilk
    Pancakes, 33
  Fresh Strawberry Scones,
    40
  Ginger Happy Face
    Cookies, 75
  Lemon Poppy Gems, 77
  Modern Mini Fruitcakes,
    88
  Oil-Free Cornmeal
    Muffins, 48
  Pineapple Frozen Yogurt,
    119
  Pink Grapefruit Sorbet,
    120
  Raisin Bran Muffins, 57
  Raspberry Linzer
    Cookies, 72
  Strawberry-Banana Ice
    Milk, 118
  Strawberry Custard Cups,
    121

Two-Berry Granita, 120
Vanilla Bean Ice Milk, 116

M
Maple sugar, 18
Mocha Almond Cake, 92, 94
Modern Mini Fruitcakes, 88
Muffins
  about, 43–44
  Banana-Walnut Muffins,
    56
  Blueberry Corn Muffins,
    45
  Blueberry–Oat Bran
    Muffins, 49
  Carrot-Pineapple Muffins,
    54
  Chocolate-Walnut Muffins,
    46
  Huckleberry-Apple
    Muffins, 50
  Oil-Free Cornmeal
    Muffins, 48
  Raisin Bran Muffins, 57
  Raspberry–Oat Flour
    Muffins, 52
  Washington State
    Blackberry Muffins, 51

N
New-Fashioned Pie Dough,
  98
"No added fat" recipes
  Apple-Cherry Cobbler,
    108
  Carrot-Pineapple Muffins,
    54
  Oil-Free Cornmeal
    Muffins, 48
  Peach–Poppy Seed
    Muffins, 55

O
Oil-Free Cornmeal
  Muffins, 48
Orange Sherbet, Blood, 119

P
Pancakes
  Banana-Nut Pancakes, 34
  Blueberry Buttermilk
    Pancakes, 33
Parfait, Tropical Fruit
  Mousse, 115
Peach Foldover Pie, 100
Peach–Poppy Seed Muffins,
  55

Peanut Butter Cookies, Red
  Hot, 76
Pear Frangipane Custard,
  104
Pear Frangipane Tart, 104
Pecans
  Apple–Pecan Praline Tart,
    102
  Baked Apples with
    Maple-Pecan Crust, 32
  Banana-Nut Pancakes, 34
  Banana-Pecan Scones, 37
  Chocolate Chip and
    Pecan Cookies, 61
  Sticky Pecan-Raisin Buns,
    26
Pie dough
  Double Crust
    New-Fashioned Pie
    Dough, 98
  New-Fashioned Pie
    Dough, 98
Pies
  about, 97
  Apple-Blueberry Double
    Crust Pie, 106
  Peach Foldover Pie, 100
  Pumpkin-Yam Pie, 107
Pineapple
  Carrot-Pineapple
    Muffins, 54
  Pineapple Frozen Yogurt,
    119
Pink Grapefruit Sorbet, 120
Prune Butter, 23
Pumpkin-Yam Pie, 107

R
Raisins
  Raisin Bran Muffins, 57
  Sticky Pecan-Raisin Buns,
    26
Raspberries
  Chocolate Raspberry
    Fortress Cake, 86–87
  Raspberry Linzer Cookies,
    72
  Raspberry–Oat Flour
    Muffins, 52
  Raspberry Tartlets, 110
  Two-Berry Granita, 120
Red Hot Peanut Butter
  Cookies, 76

S
Scones
  about, 36
  Banana-Pecan Scones, 37
  Barley-Currant Scones, 41
    38

Cranberry-Walnut
  Scones 38
Fresh Strawberry Scones,
  40
Sherbet, Blood Orange, 119
Shortbread, Almond, 74
Shortcakes, Strawberry, 95
Sorbet, Pink Grapefruit, 120
Southern-style Cornmeal
  Waffles, 29
Soy milk
  about, 22
  Soy Milk Truffles, 124
Sticky Pecan-Raisin Buns, 26
Strawberries
  Fresh Strawberry Scones,
    40
  Fresh Strawberry Tartlets,
    110
  Strawberry-Banana Ice
    Milk, 118
  Strawberry Custard Cups,
    121
  Strawberry Sauce, 95
  Strawberry Shortcakes, 95
Sugar-Free Truffles, 122, 124
Sweeteners, 16–18

T

Tarts and tartlets
  Apple–Pecan Praline Tart,
    102
  Apple Tart, 103
  Blueberry Tartlets, 110
  Fresh Strawberry Tartlets,
    110
  Lemon Meringue Tartlets,
    111
  Pear Frangipane Tart, 104
  Raspberry Tartlets, 110
Tofu
  about, 22
  Pumpkin-Yam Pie, 107
  Tropical Fruit Mousse
    Parfait, 115
Tropical Fruit Mousse
  Parfait, 115
Truffles, Sugar-Free, 122,
  124
Turnovers, Apple, 99
Two-Berry Granita, 120

V

Vanilla Bean Ice Milk, 116

W

Waffles, Southern-style
  Cornmeal, 29

Walnuts
  Banana-Walnut Muffins,
    56
  Black Forest Bundt Cake,
    82
  Chocolate-Walnut Muffins,
    46
  Chocolate-Walnut
    Topping, 90
  Cranberry-Walnut Scones,
    38
Washington State Blackberry
  Muffins, 51
Wheat-free recipes
  Apple Tart, 103
  Barley-Currant Scones, 41
  Chocolate-dipped Barley
    Cookies, 64
  Granola Triple Oat
    Cookies, 65
  Raspberry Linzer Cookies,
    72
  Raspberry–Oat Flour
    Muffins, 52
  Strawberry Custard Cups,
    121
  Sugar-Free Truffles, 122,
    124
Whole-grain recipes
  Almond Jewel Cookies, 69
  Applesauce-Currant
    Cookies, 68
  Banana Layer Cake, 83
  Banana-Nut Pancakes, 34
  Banana-Walnut Muffins,
    56
  Blackberry Upside-Down
    Cake, 84
  Black Forest Bundt Cake,
    82
  Blueberry Buttermilk
    Pancakes, 33
  Blueberry–Oat Bran
    Muffins, 49
  Carrot-Pineapple Muffins,
    54
  Chocolate Chip and
    Pecan Cookies, 61
  Chocolate-Walnut
    Muffins, 46
  Coconut Macaroons, 71
  Faux-Nuts, 28
  Ginger Happy Face
    Cookies, 75
  Granola Triple Oat
    Cookies, 65
  Lemon Meringue Tartlets,
    111
  Lemon Poppy Gems, 77
  Modern Mini Fruitcakes,
    88

Peach–Poppy Seed
  Muffins, 55
Raisin Bran Muffins, 57
Red Hot Peanut Butter
  Cookies, 76

Y

Yam Pie, Pumpkin, 107
Yogurt, Pineapple Frozen,
  119

Table of Equivalents

The exact equivalents in the following tables have been rounded for convenience.

US/UK

oz=ounce
lb=pound
in=inch
ft=foot
tbl=tablespoon
fl oz=fluid ounce
qt=quart

Metric

g=gram
kg=kilogram
mm=millimeter
cm=centimeter
ml=milliliter
l=liter

Weights

US/UK	Metric
1 oz	30 g
2 oz	60 g
3 oz	90 g
4 oz (¼ lb)	125 g
5 oz (⅓ lb)	155 g
6 oz	185 g
7 oz	220 g
8 oz (½ lb)	250 g
10 oz	315 g
12 oz (¾ lb)	375 g
14 oz	440 g
16 oz (1 lb)	500 g
1½ lb	750 g
2 lb	1 kg
3 lb	1.5 kg

Length Measures

⅛ in	3 mm
¼ in	6 mm
½ in	12 mm
1 in	2.5 cm
2 in	5 cm
3 in	7.5 cm
4 in	10 cm
5 in	13 cm
6 in	15 cm
7 in	18 cm
8 in	20 cm
9 in	23 cm
10 in	25 cm
11 in	28 cm
12 in/1 ft	30 cm

Oven Temperatures

Fahrenheit	Celsius	Gas
250	120	½
275	140	1
300	150	2
325	160	3
350	180	4
375	190	5
400	200	6
425	220	7
450	230	8
475	240	9
500	260	10

Liquids

US	Metric	UK
2 tbl	30 ml	1 fl oz
¼ cup	60 ml	2 fl oz
⅓ cup	80 ml	3 fl oz
½ cup	125 ml	4 fl oz
⅔ cup	160 ml	5 fl oz
¾ cup	180 ml	6 fl oz
1 cup	250 ml	8 fl oz
1½ cups	375 ml	12 fl oz
2 cups	500 ml	16 fl oz
4 c/1 qt	1 liter	32 fl oz